ROUND BEND PRESS BOOKS

Rust: Numerous Forms of Fire

Photographs

Charles Lucas

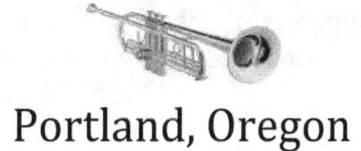

Portland, Oregon

All rights reserved. No part of this book may be reproduced in any form by any means electronic or mechanical, including photocopying, recording or by any information storage and retrieval systems, without written permission of the publisher or author except where permitted by law.

Copyright 2016 by Charles Lucas

Round Bend Press Books
1115 S.W. 11th Ave.
Portland, Oregon 97205

Designed by Terry Simons

First Edition Published 2018

ISBN: 978-1725701595

Photography—the Pacific Northwest
Published in the USA

Cover: Rust, by Charles Lucas

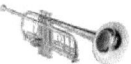

roundbendpressbooks.blogspot.com
roundbendpress@yahoo.com

Introduction

I've known Portland, Oregon artist/photographer/ceramicist Charles Lucas since before Jesus died, or so it feels like at times.

I like his work for many reasons. Most significantly, he exemplifies everything I like about artists who have captured the creative process and the making of transcendent work.

He makes it look easy, but we all know it's never easy to make great photos.

This book of photographs is Lucas' second for Round Bend Press Books, following 2011's *Ubiquitous Serpentine*, a photo collection of his paintings on ceramic.

Simple in their beauty but bold in their composition, these images turn rust into pure gold.

The artist submitted this collection after a long gestation. I welcome it because it is filled with beautiful rust and a spirit that disobeys convention and the ordinary.

Terry Simons
Founder & Publisher
Round Bend Press Books
Portland, Oregon

"Beauty can be seen in all things, seeing and composing the beauty is what separates the snapshot from the photograph."— **Matt Hardy**

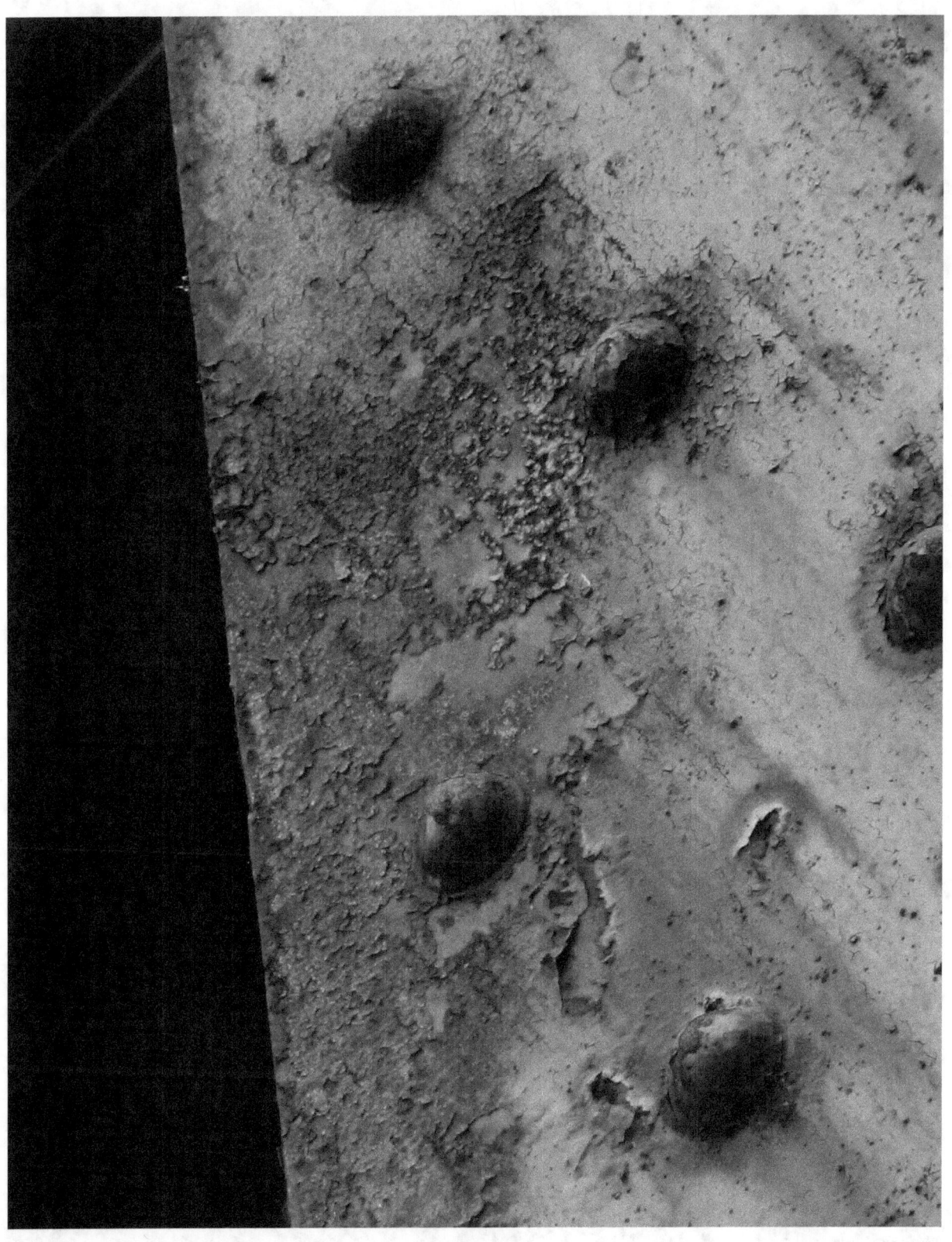

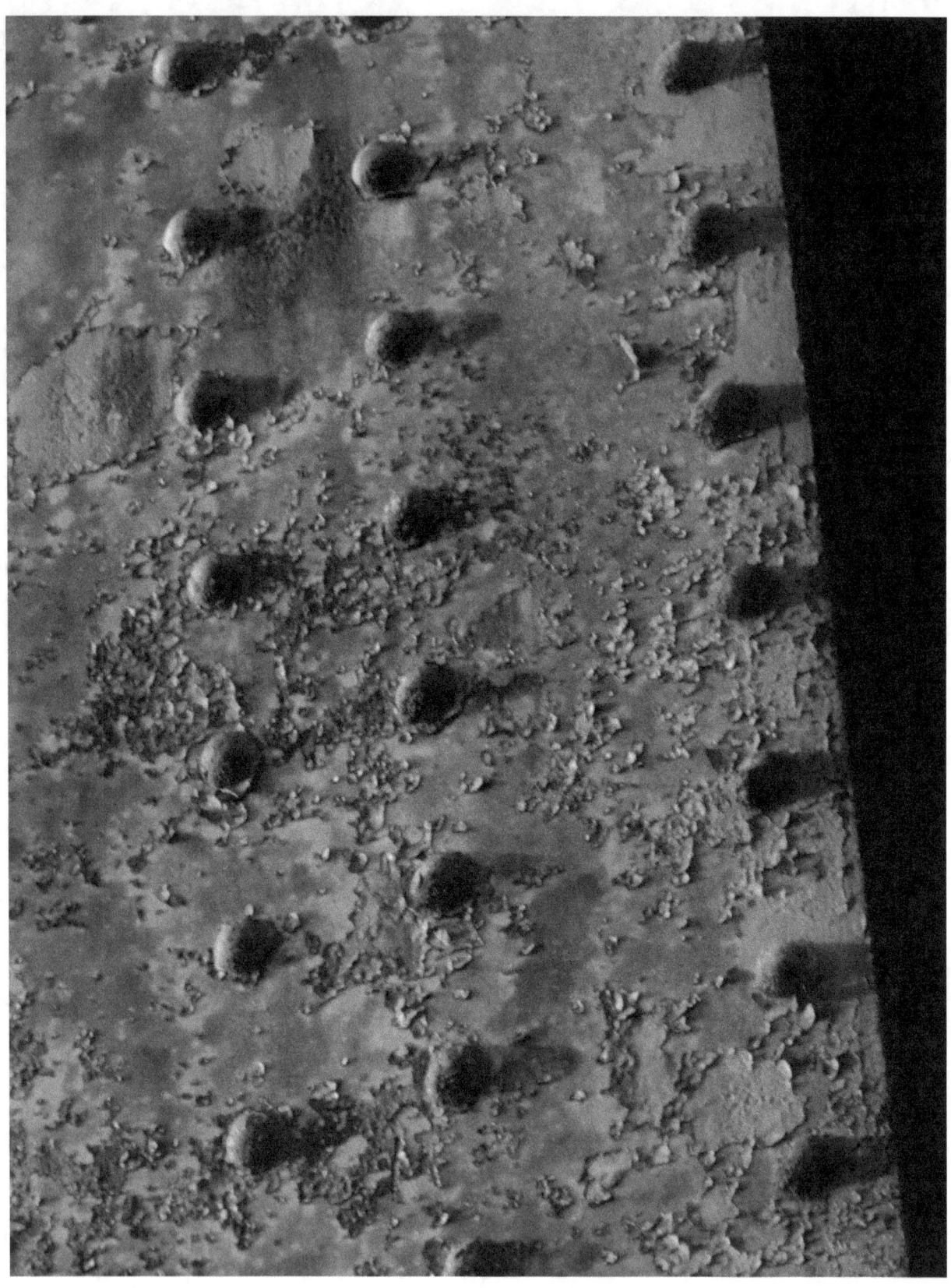

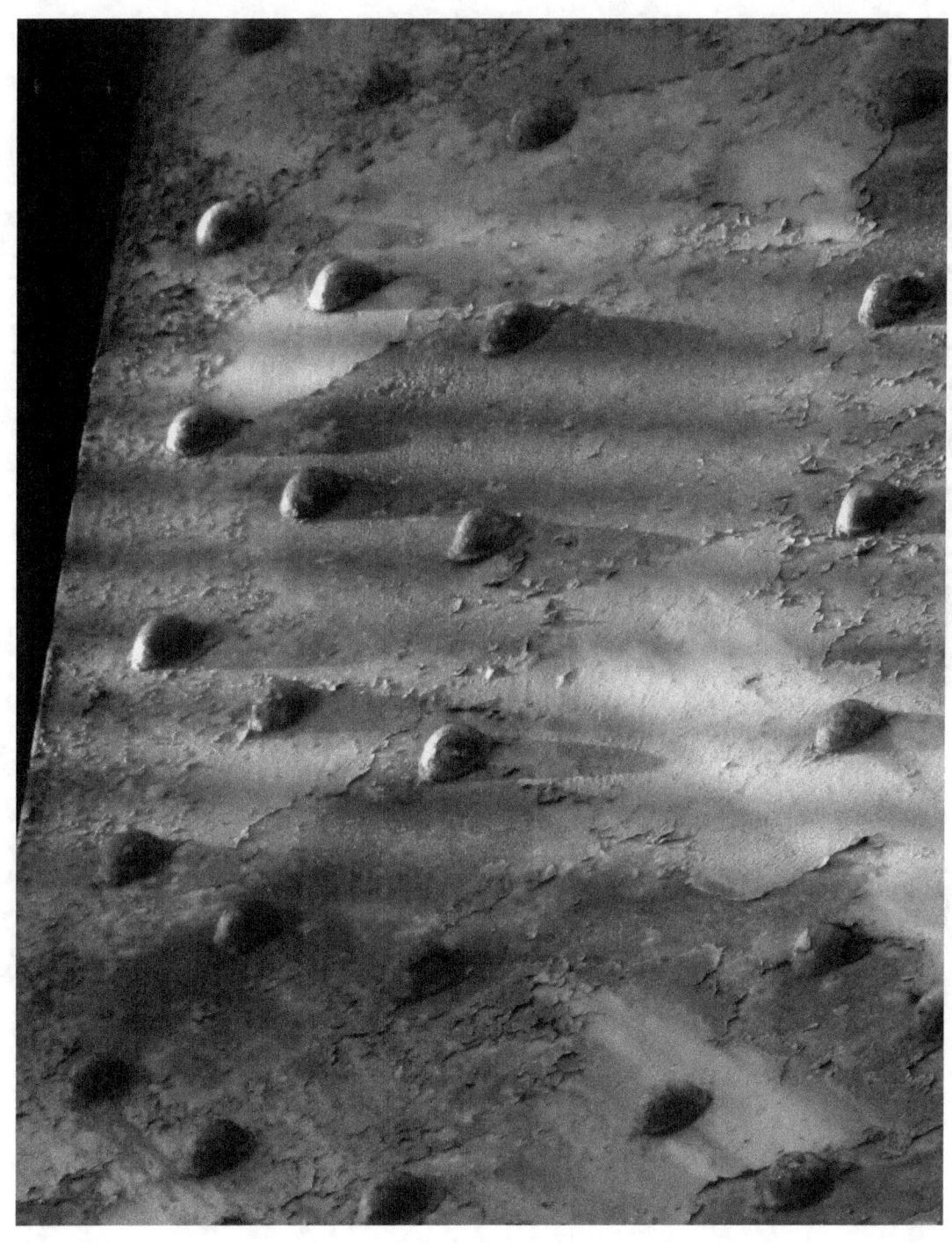

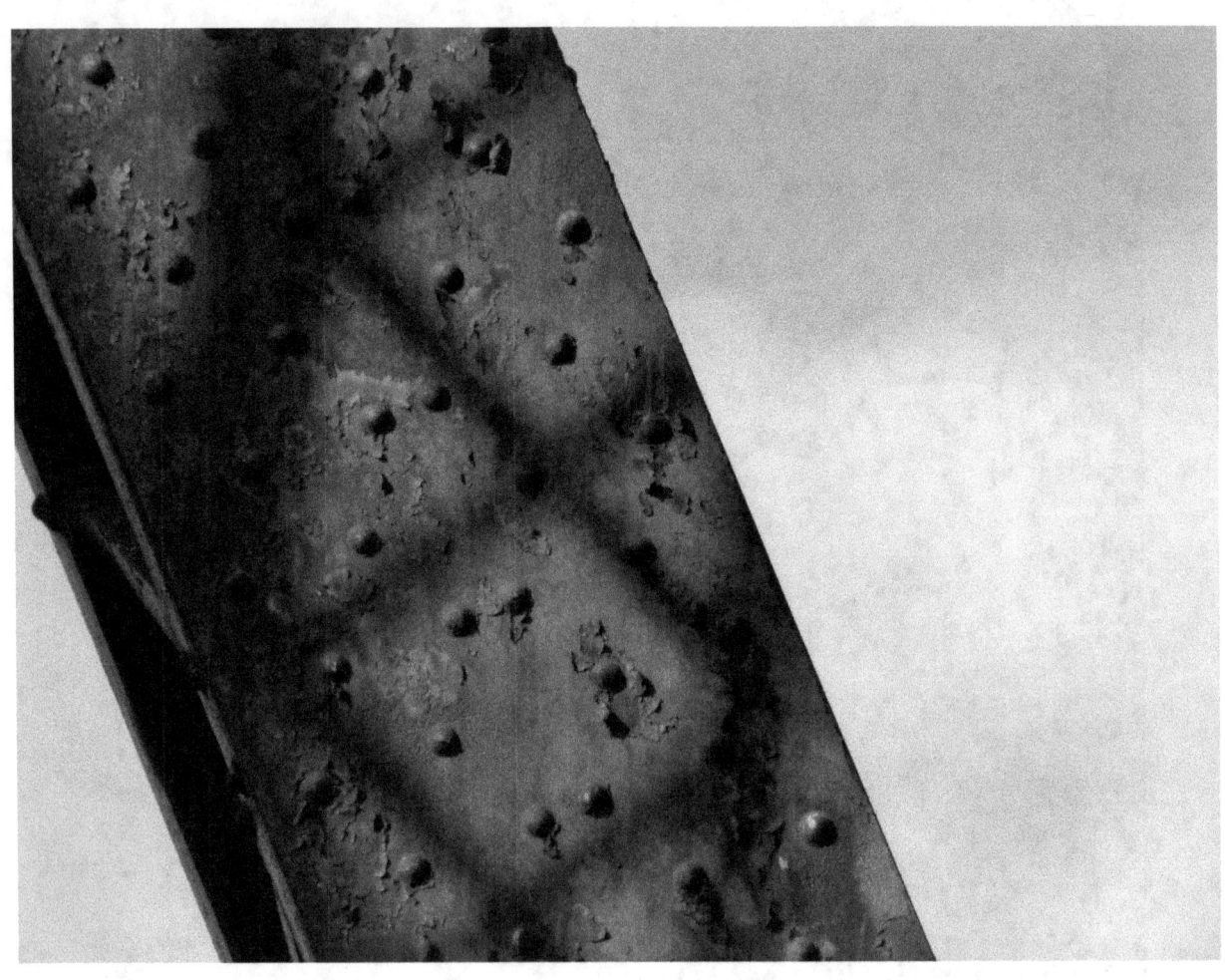

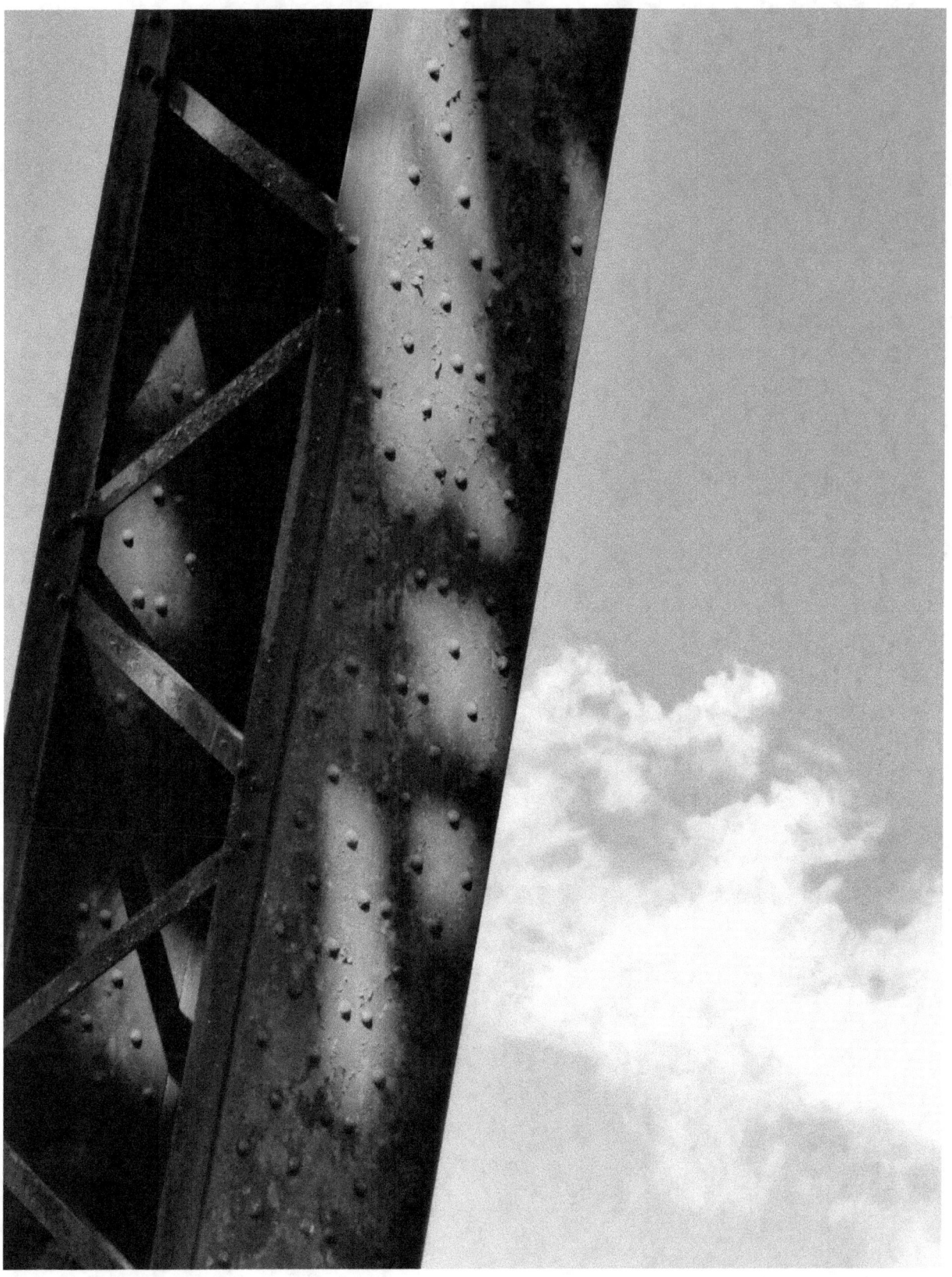

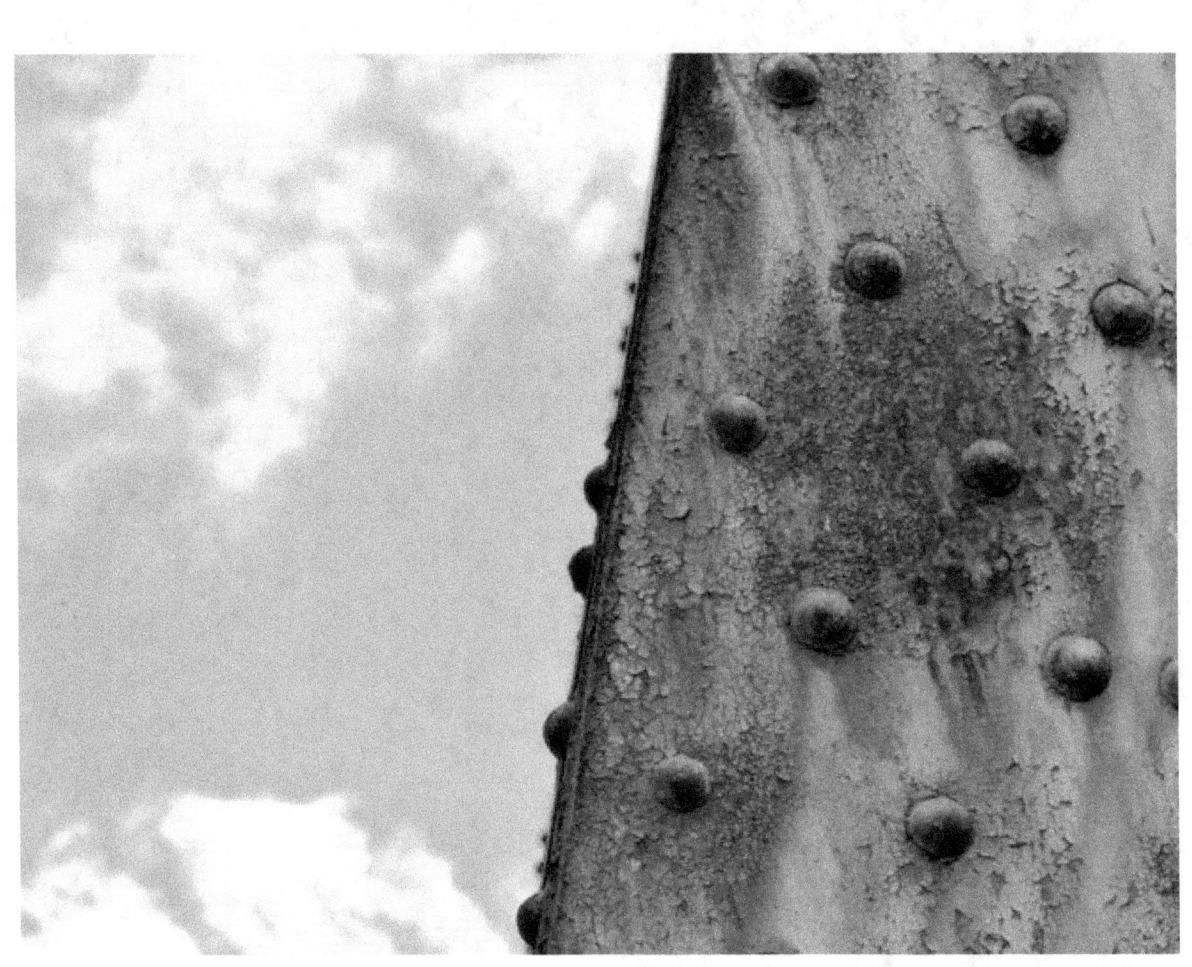

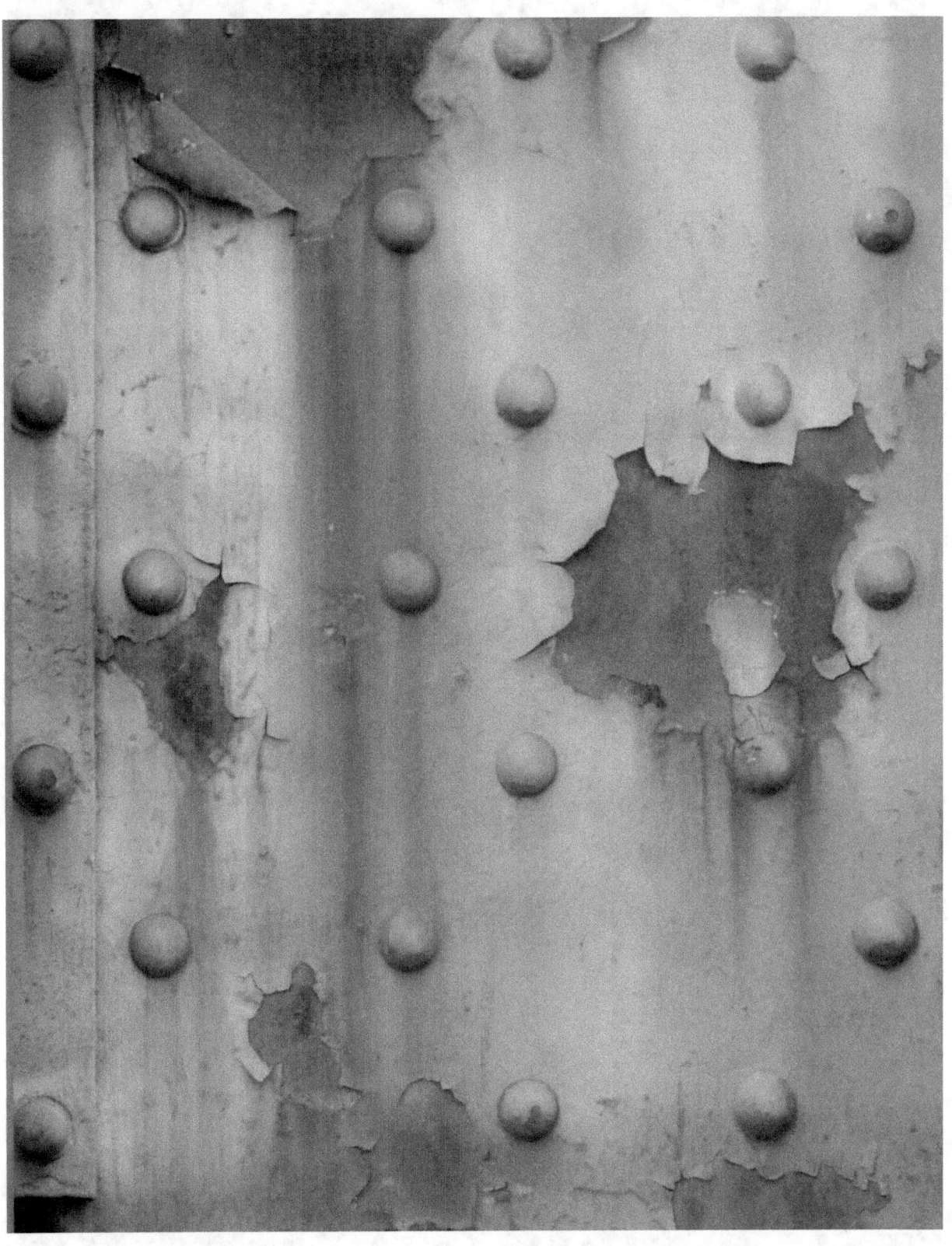

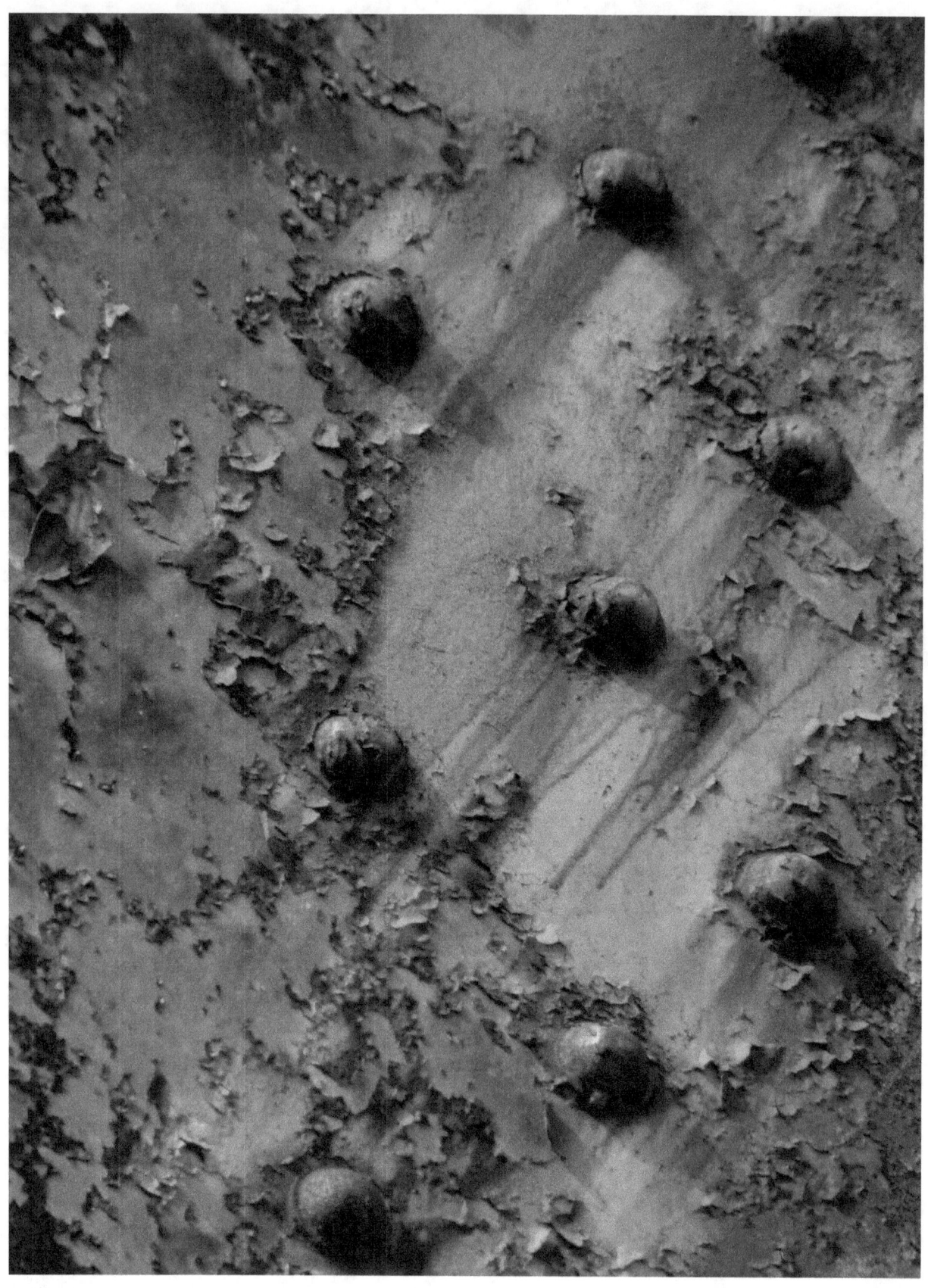

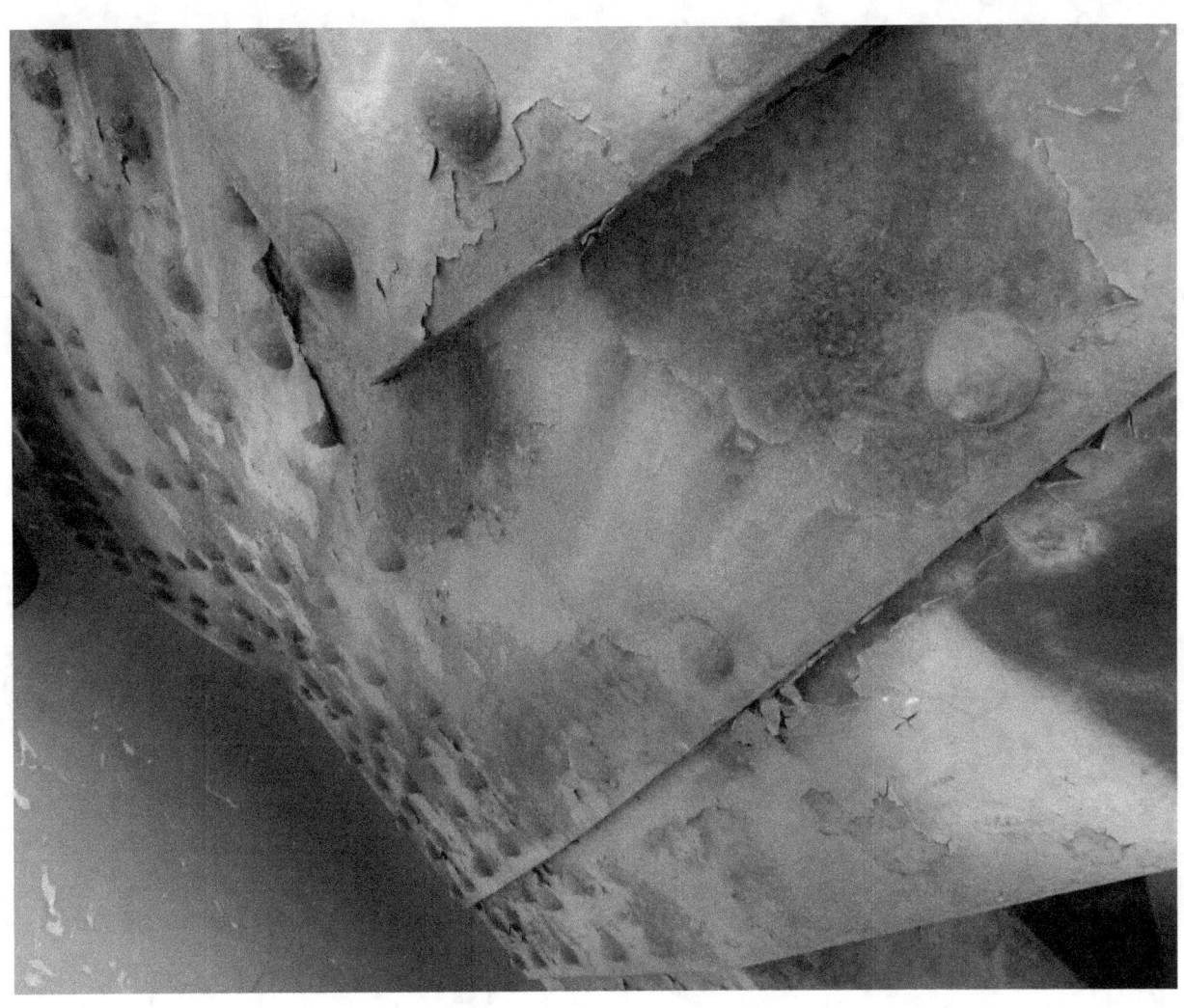

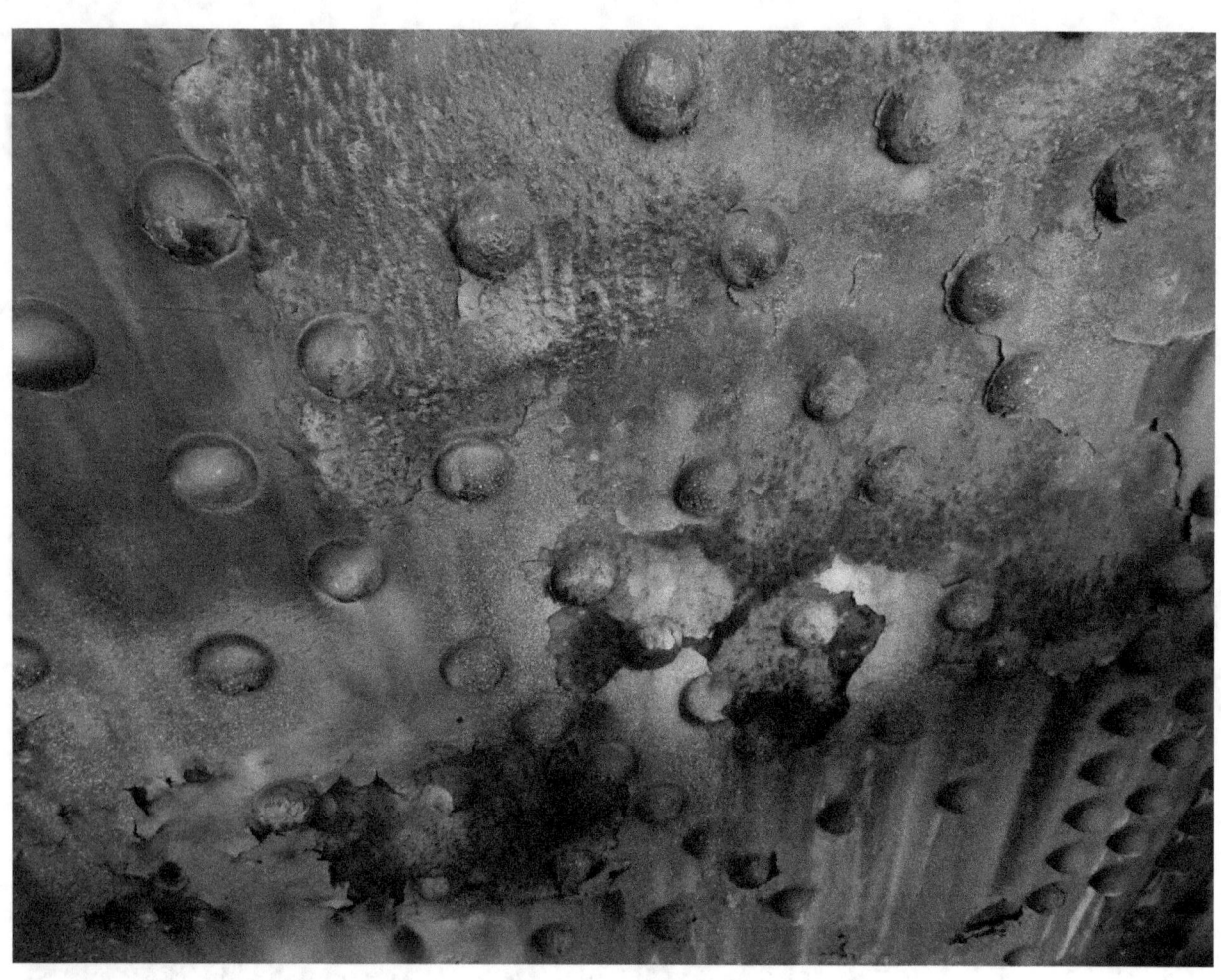

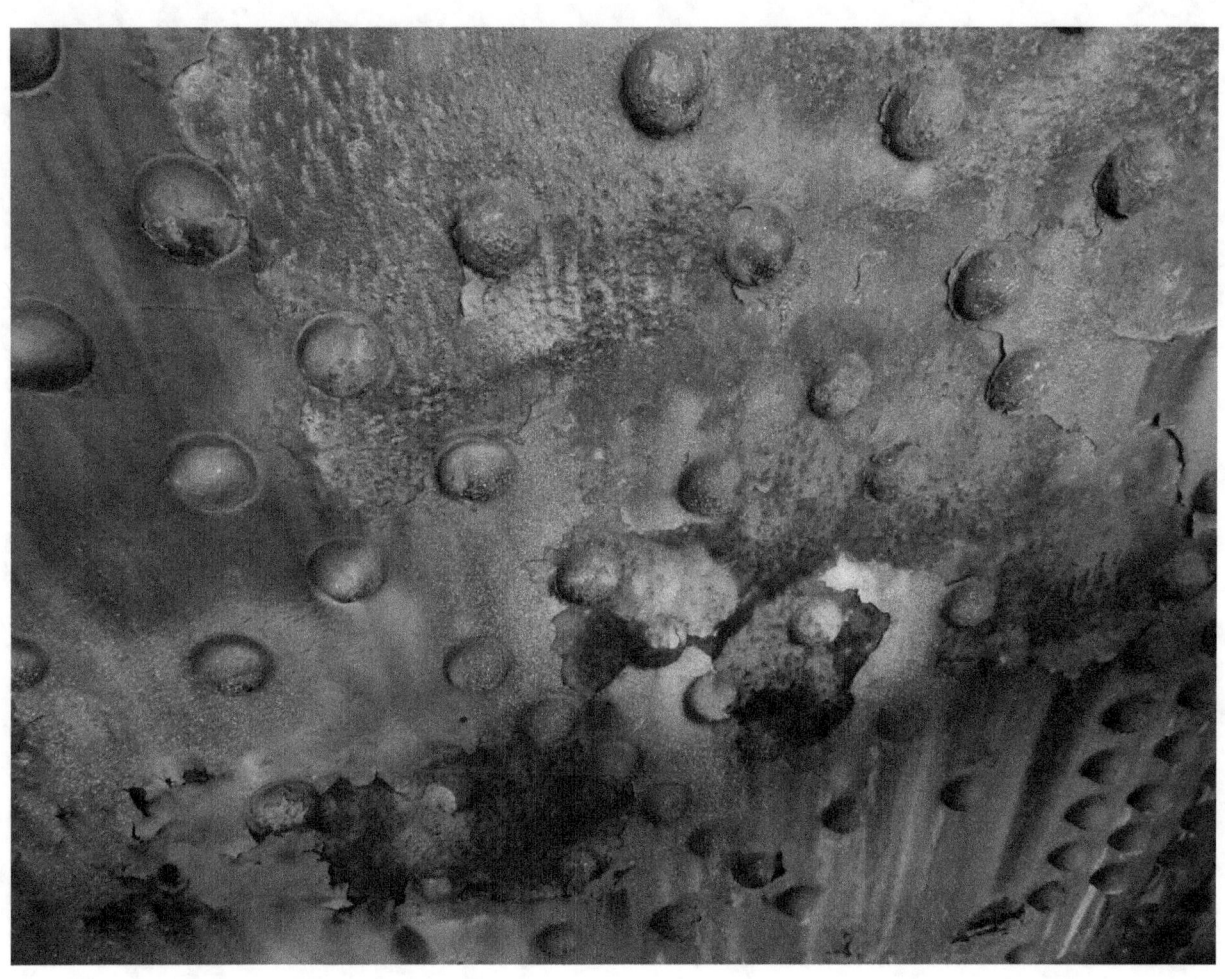

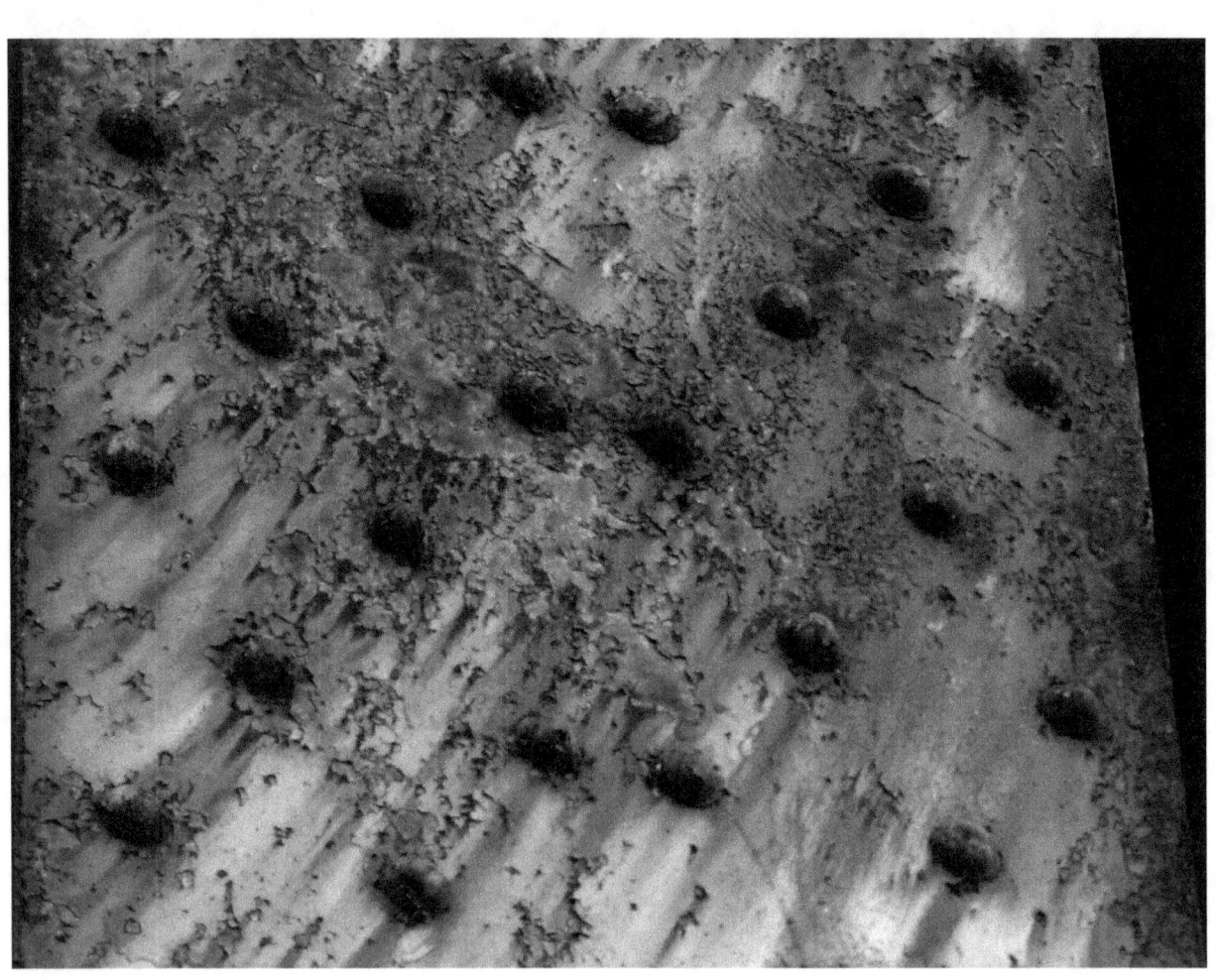

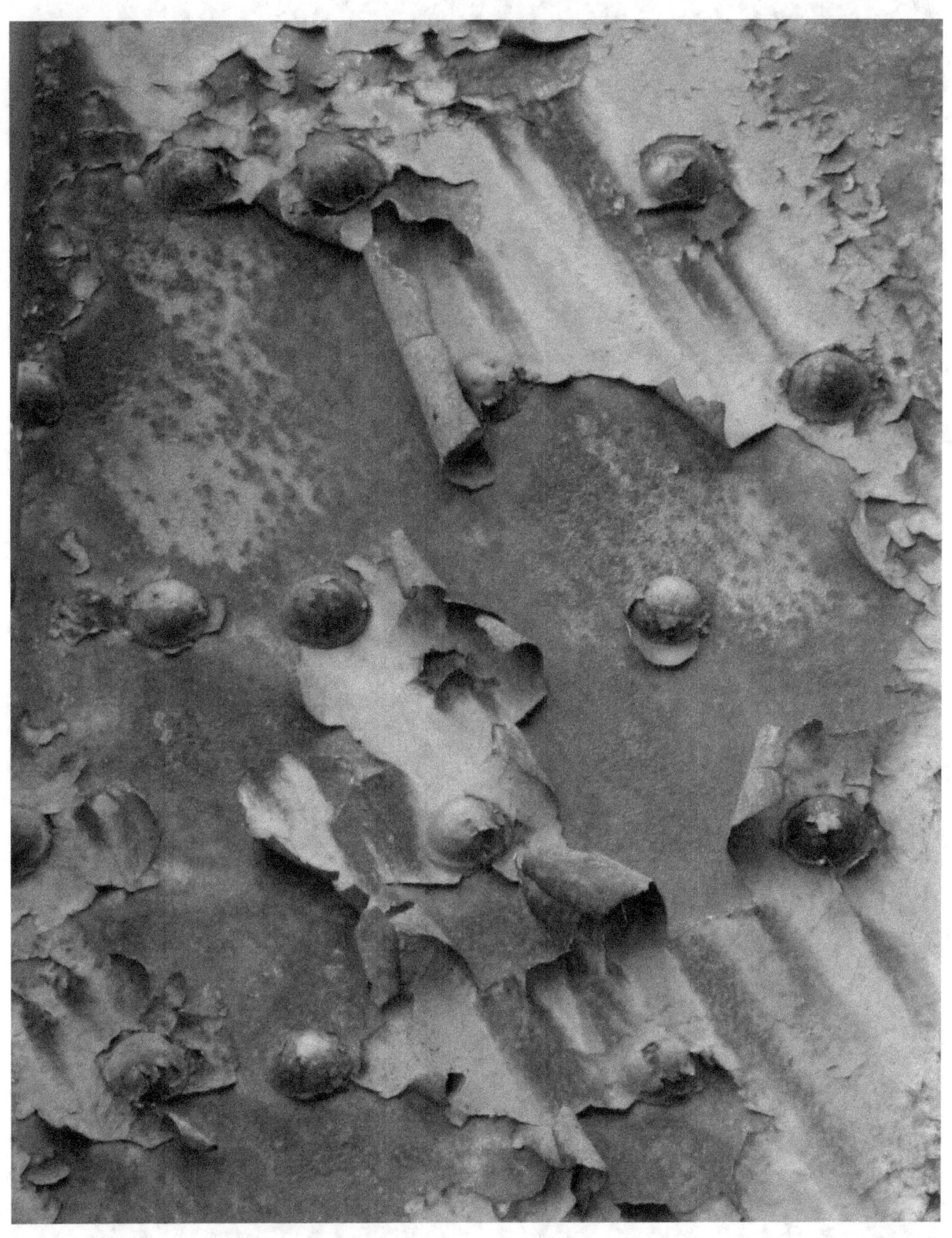

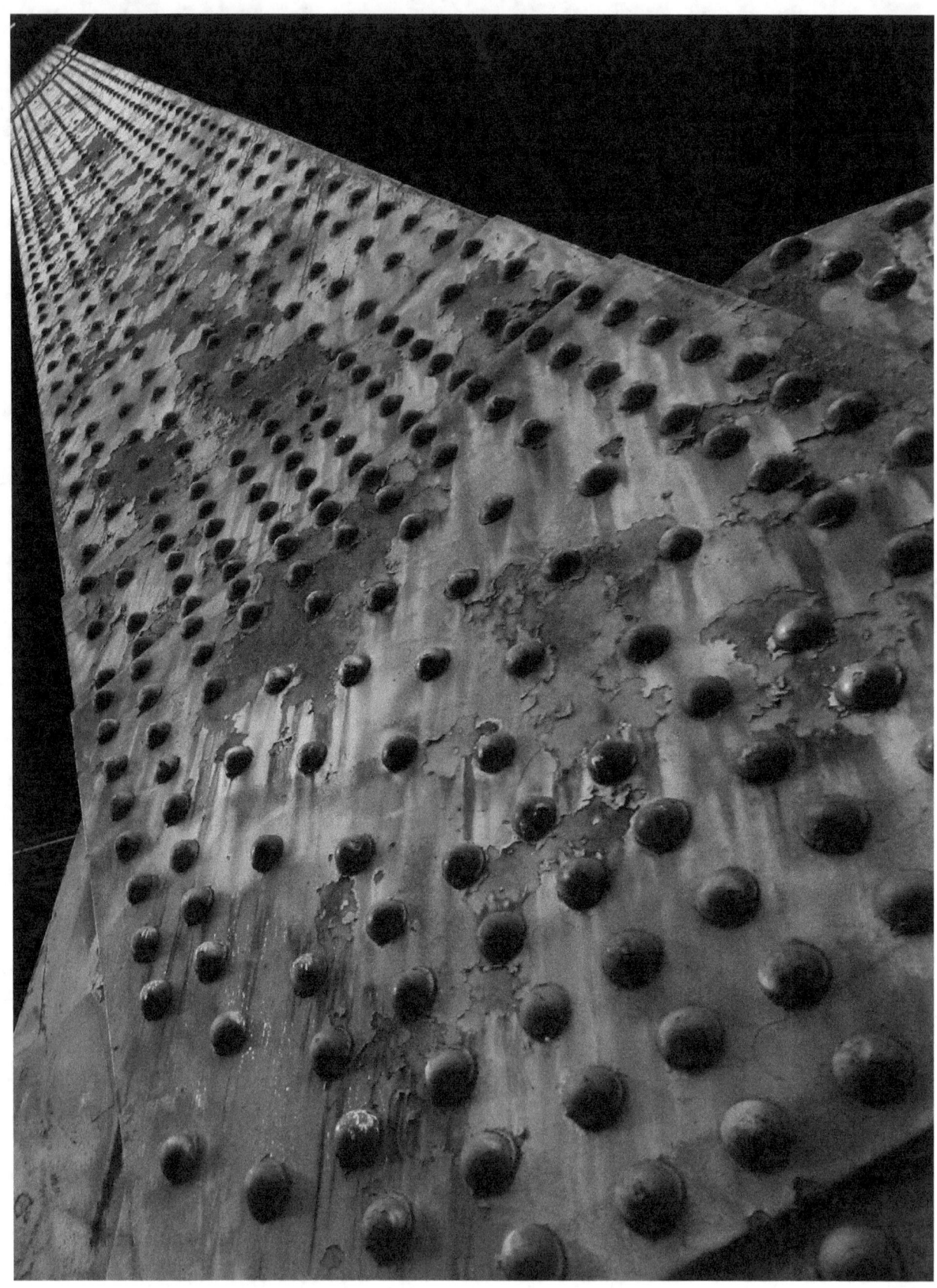

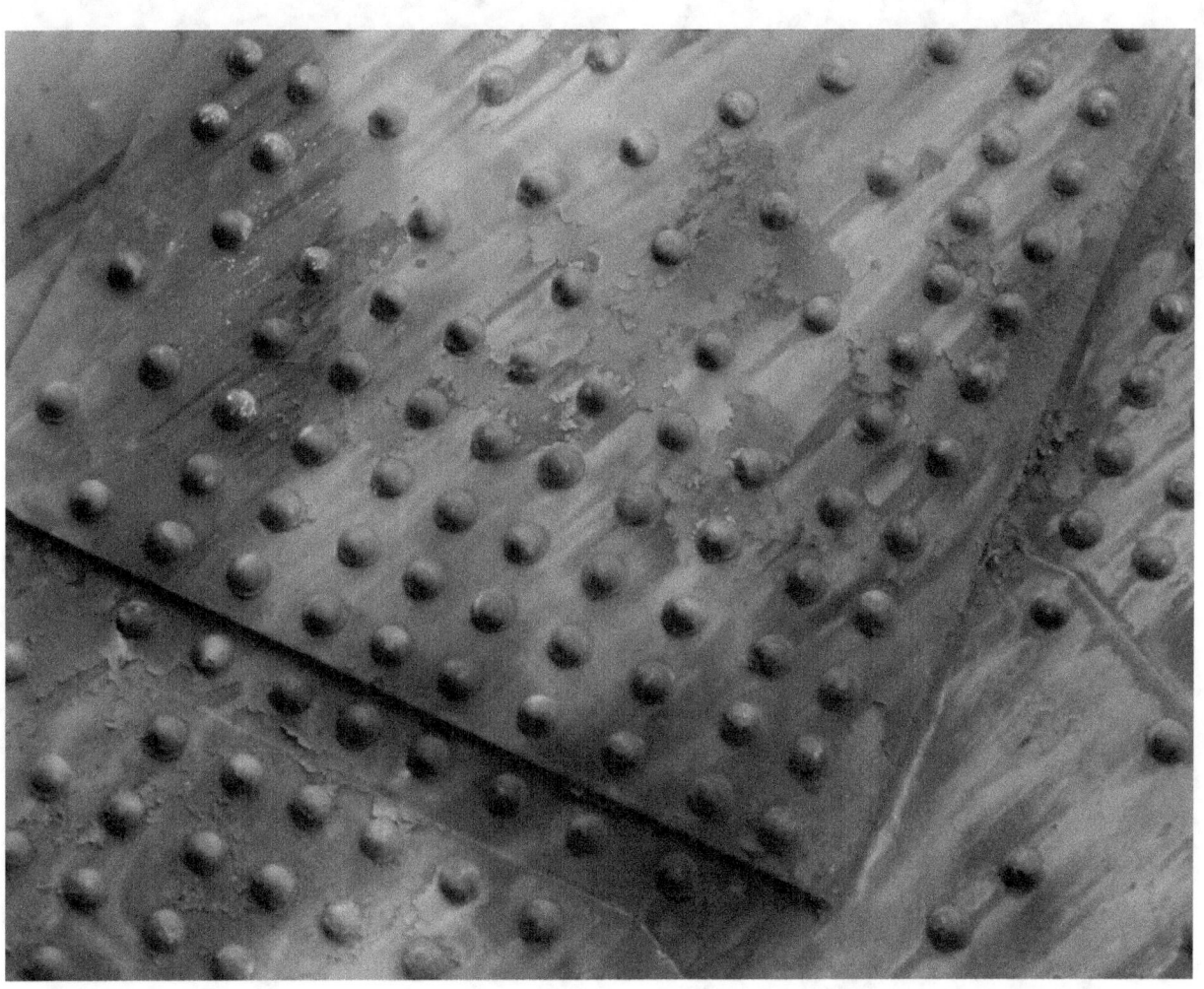

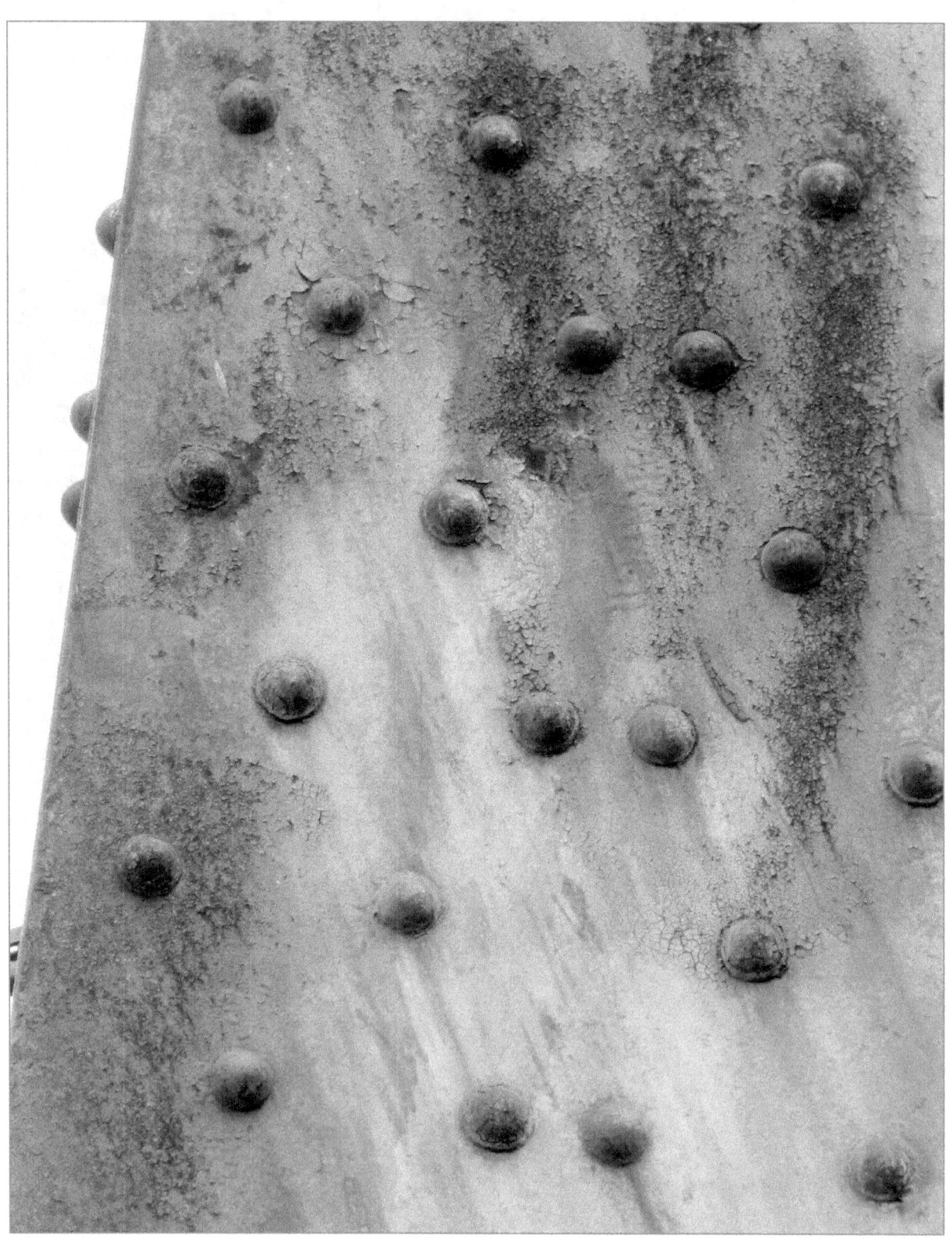

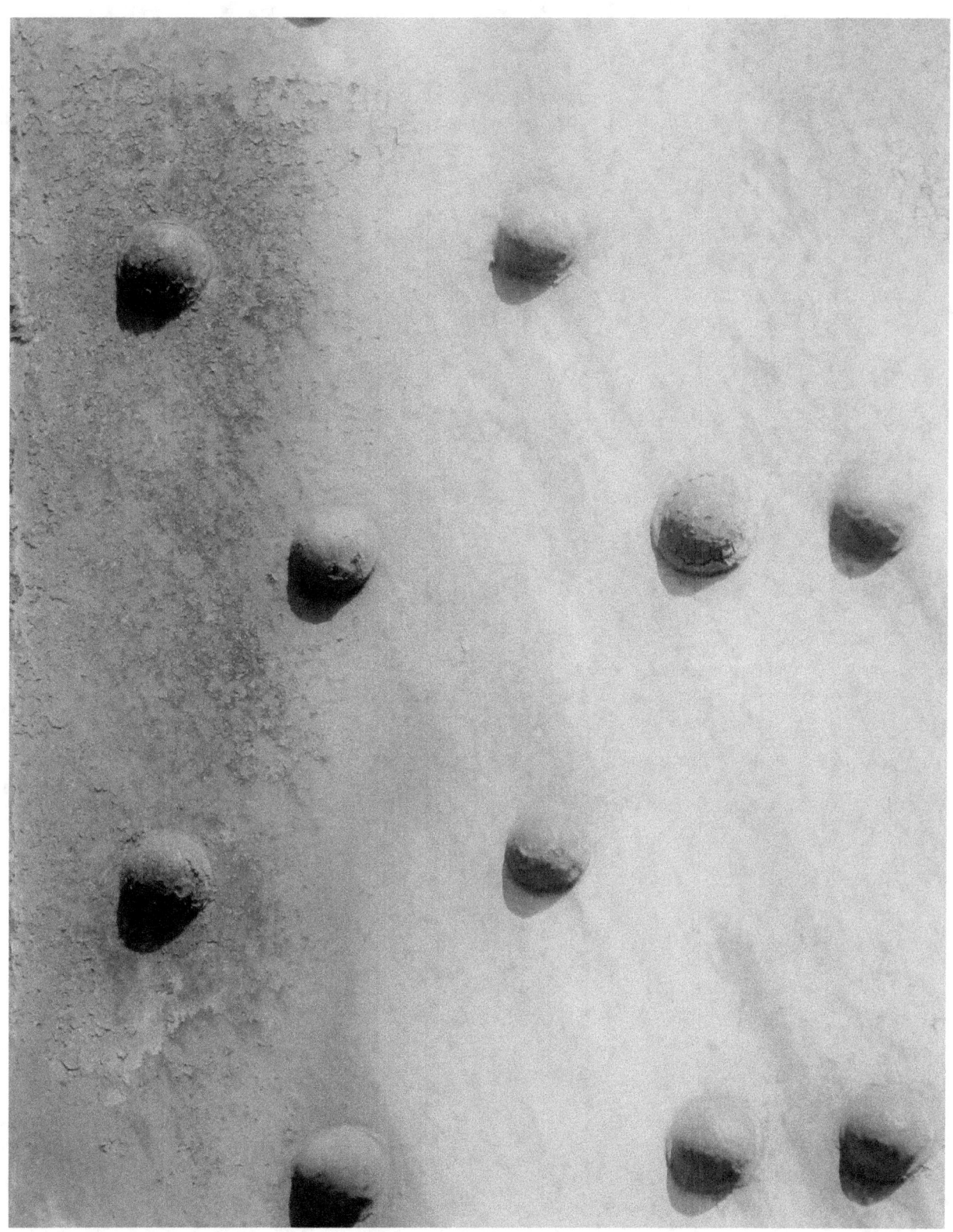

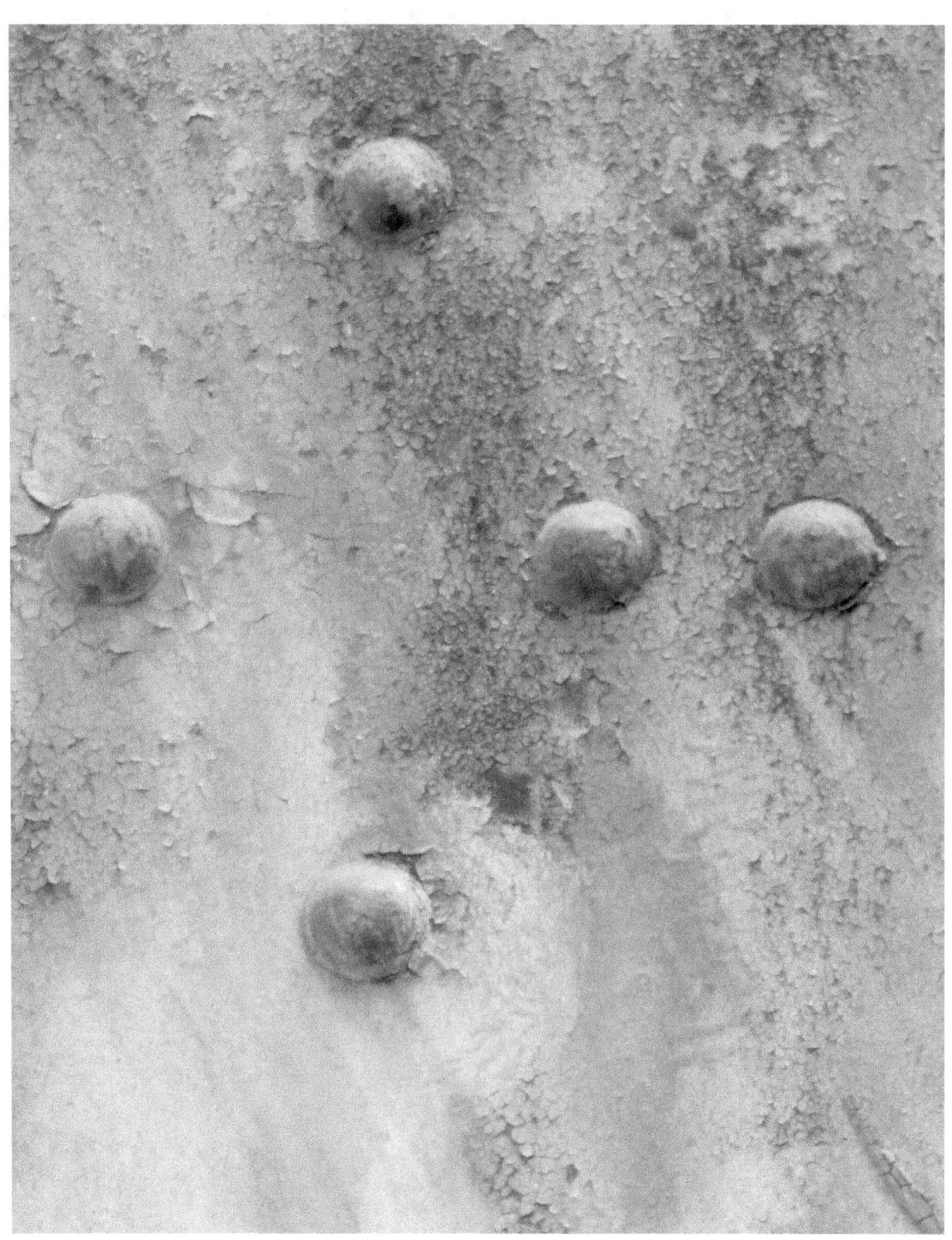

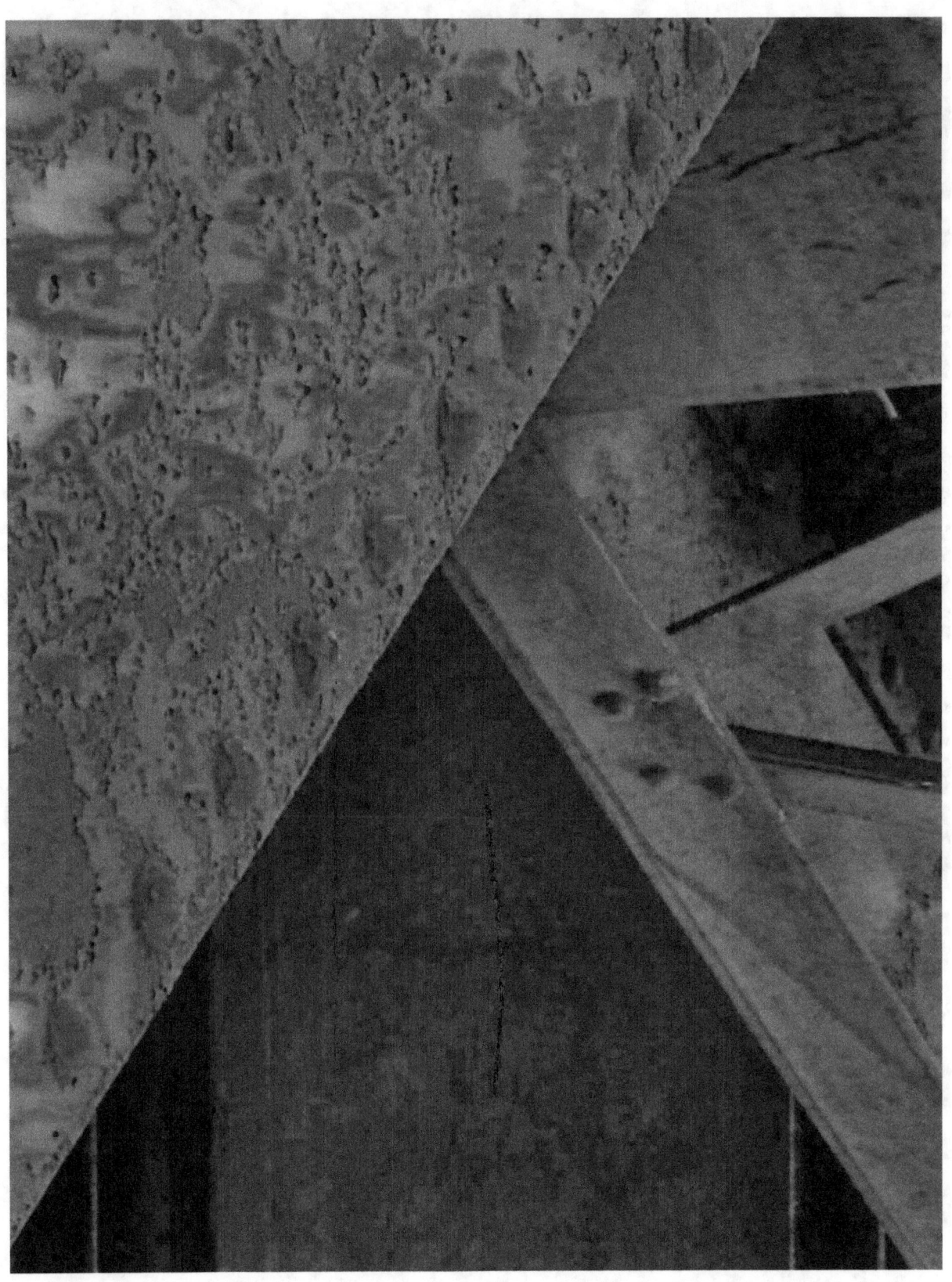

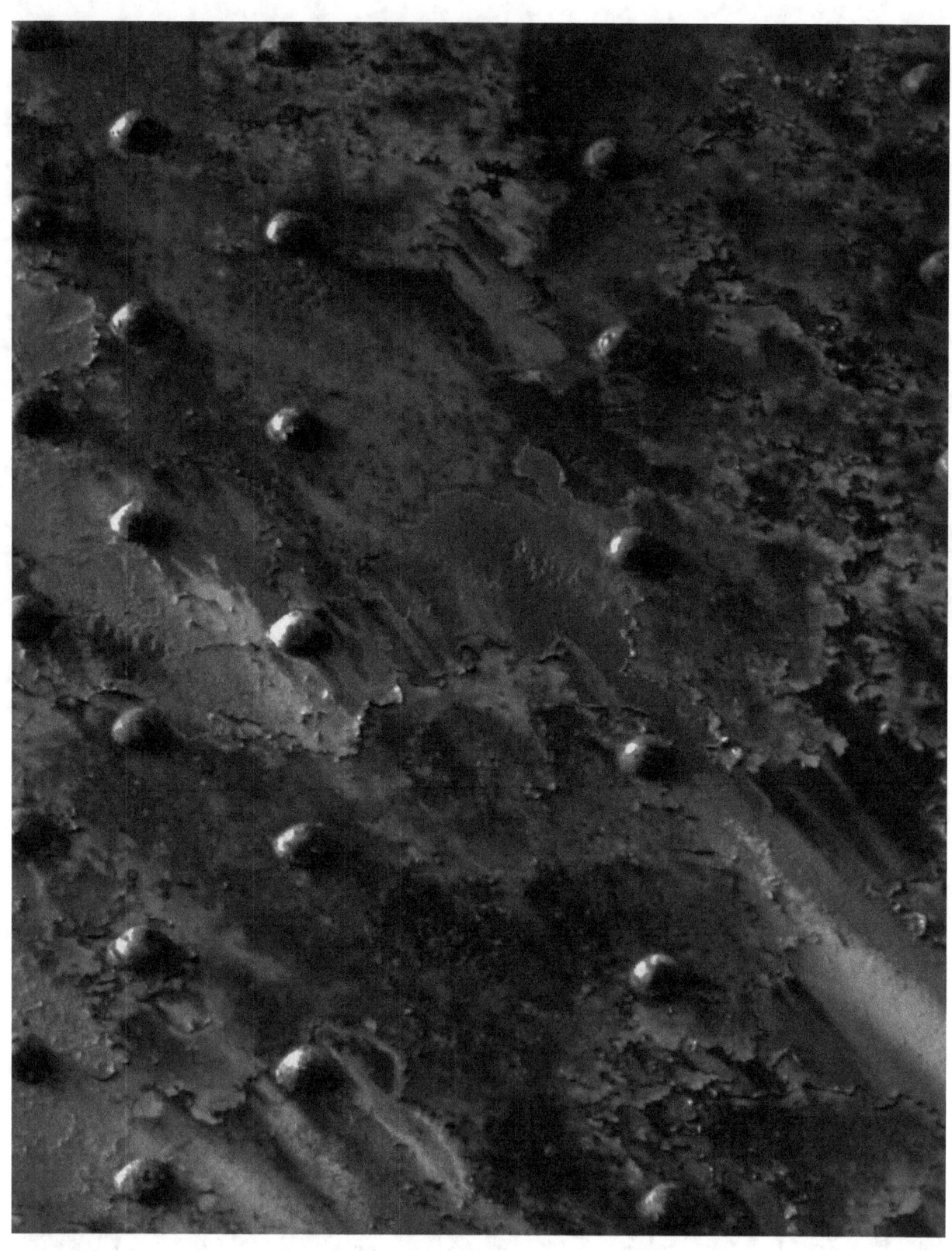

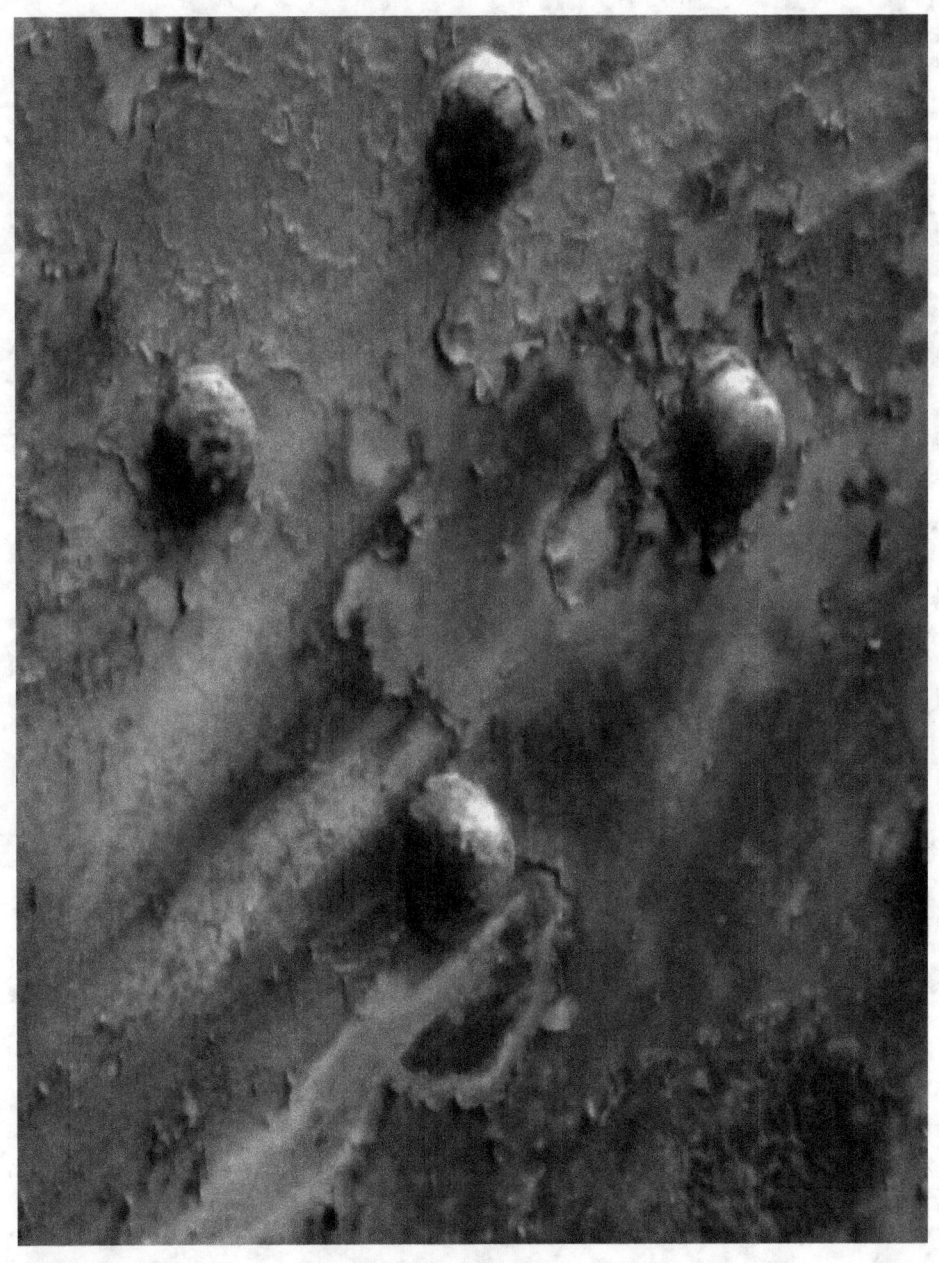

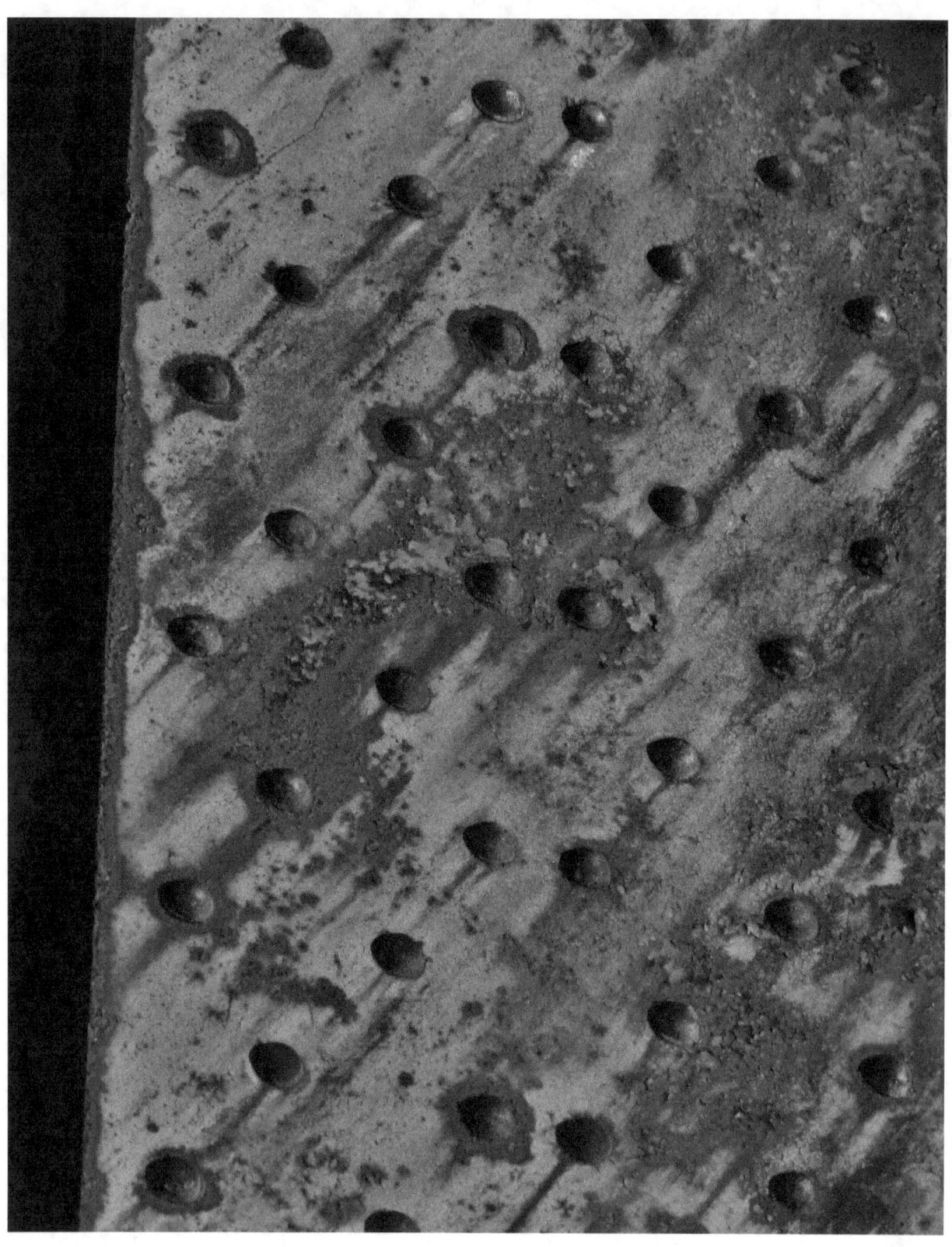

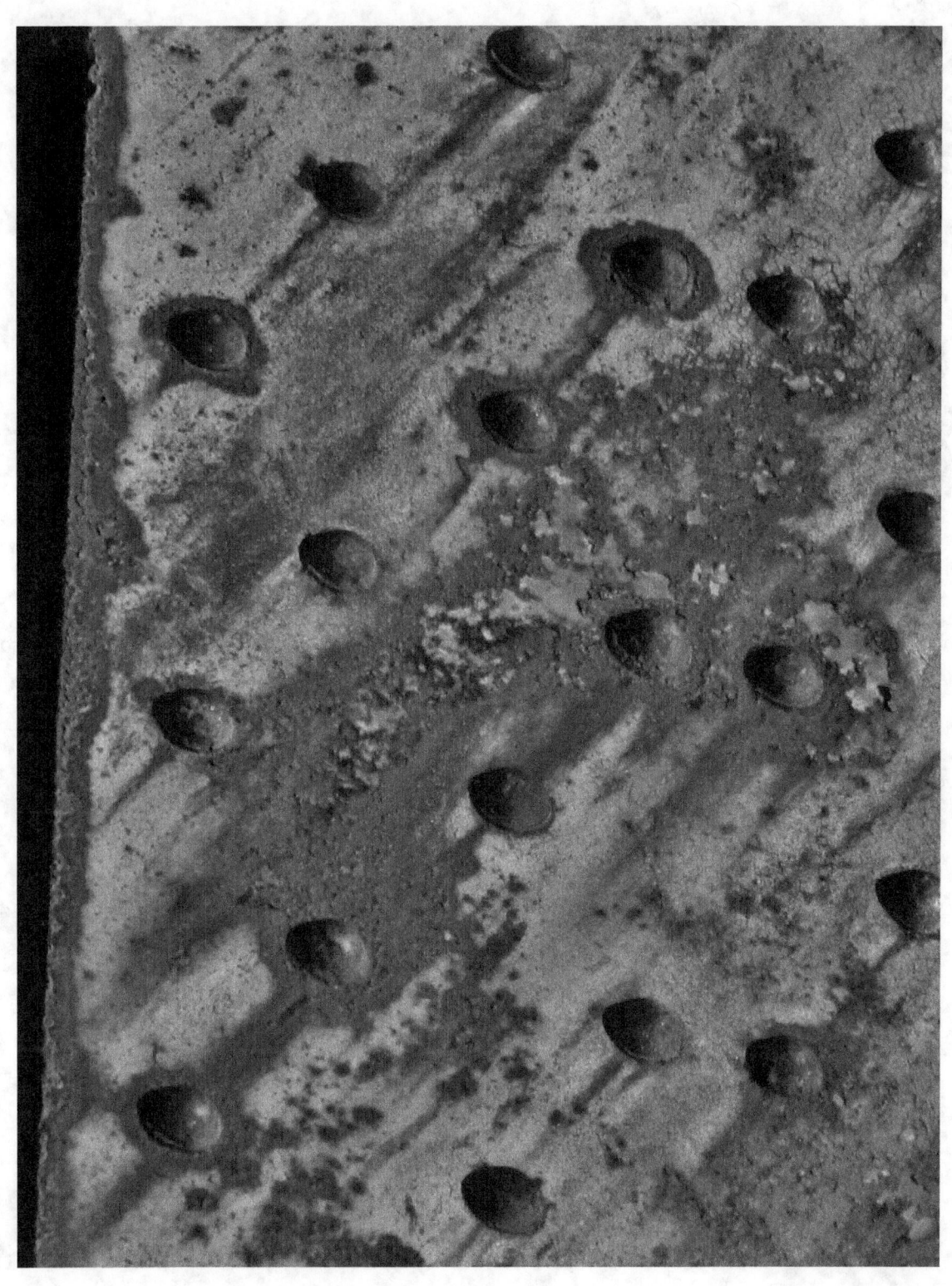

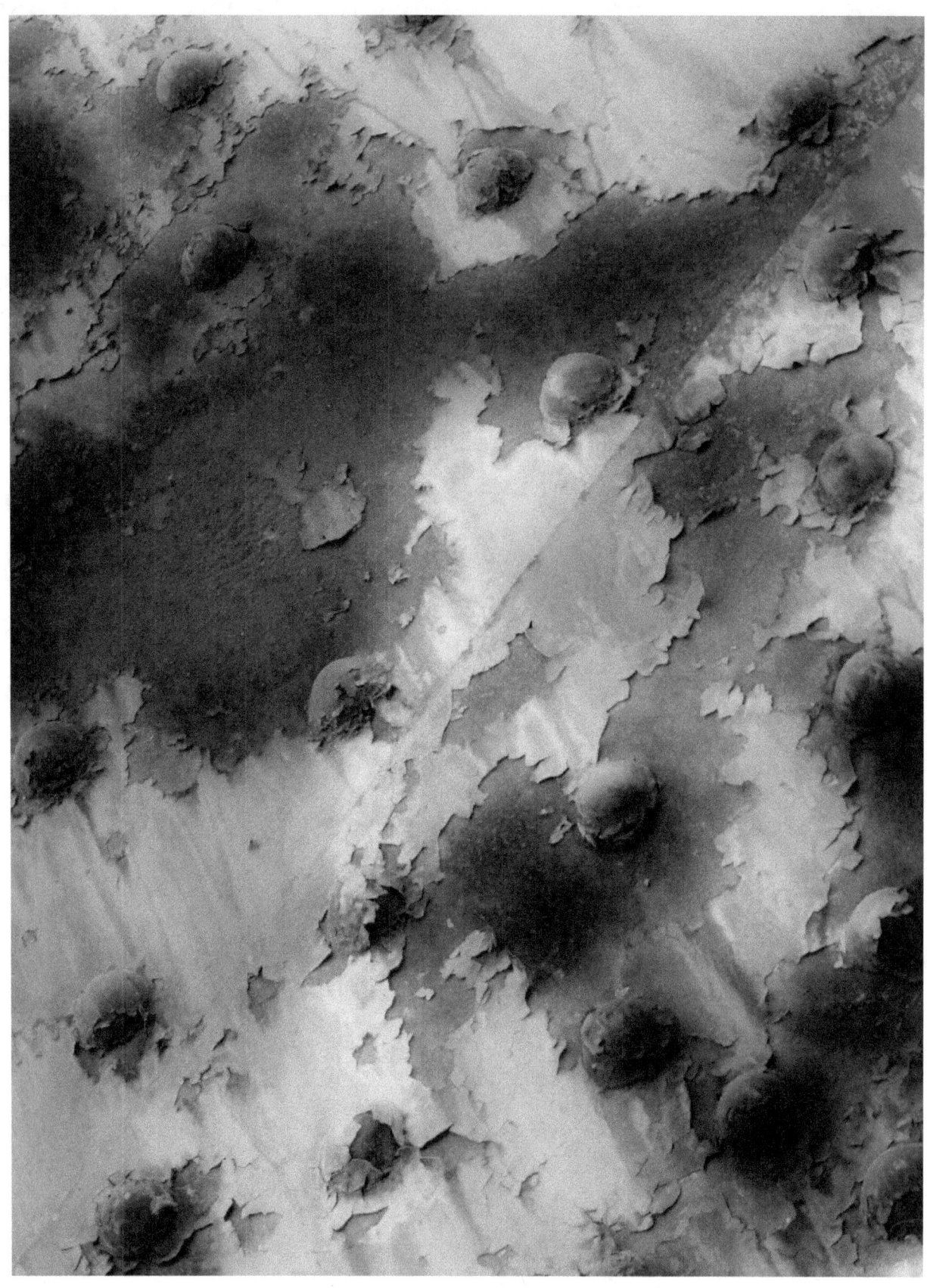

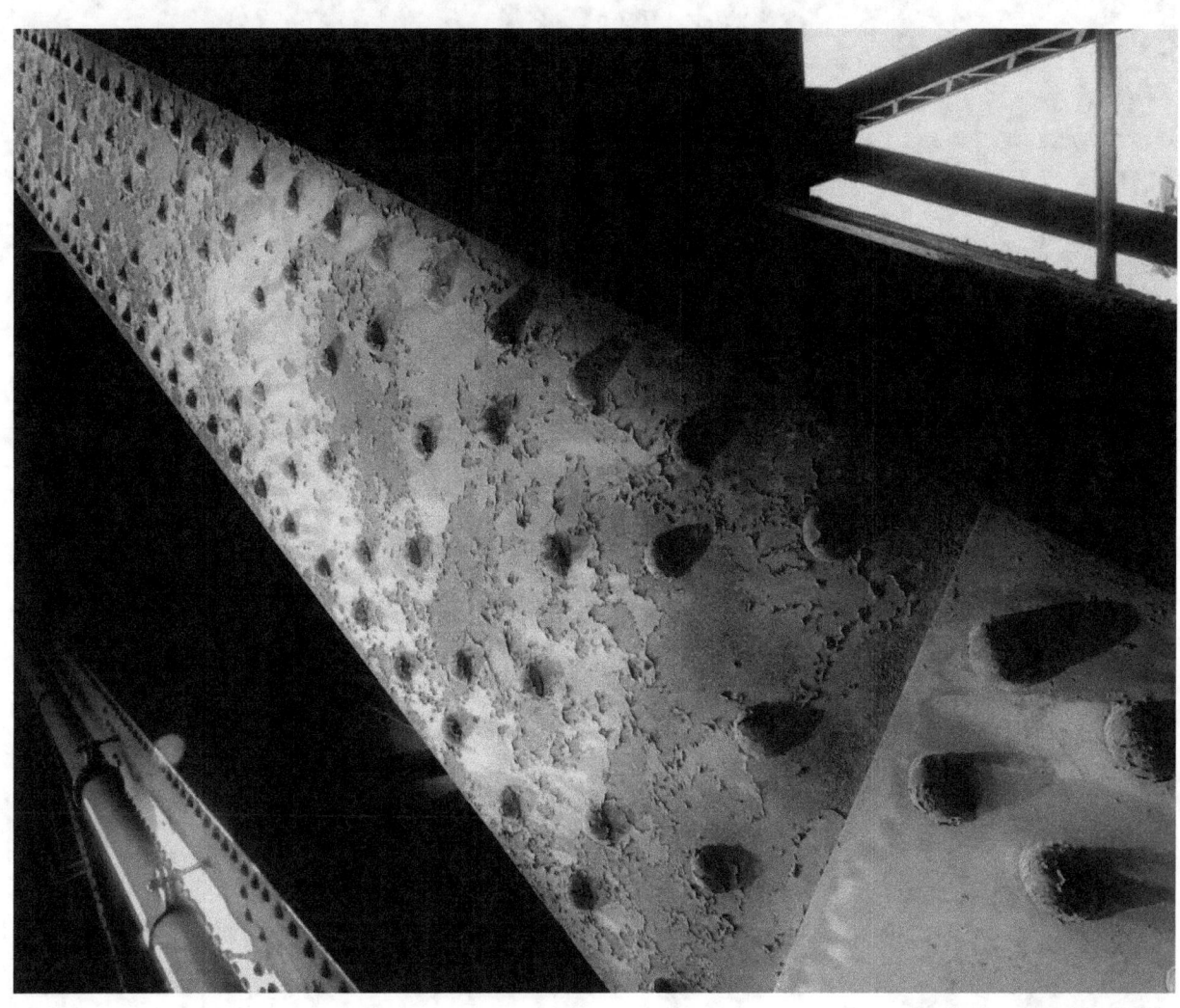

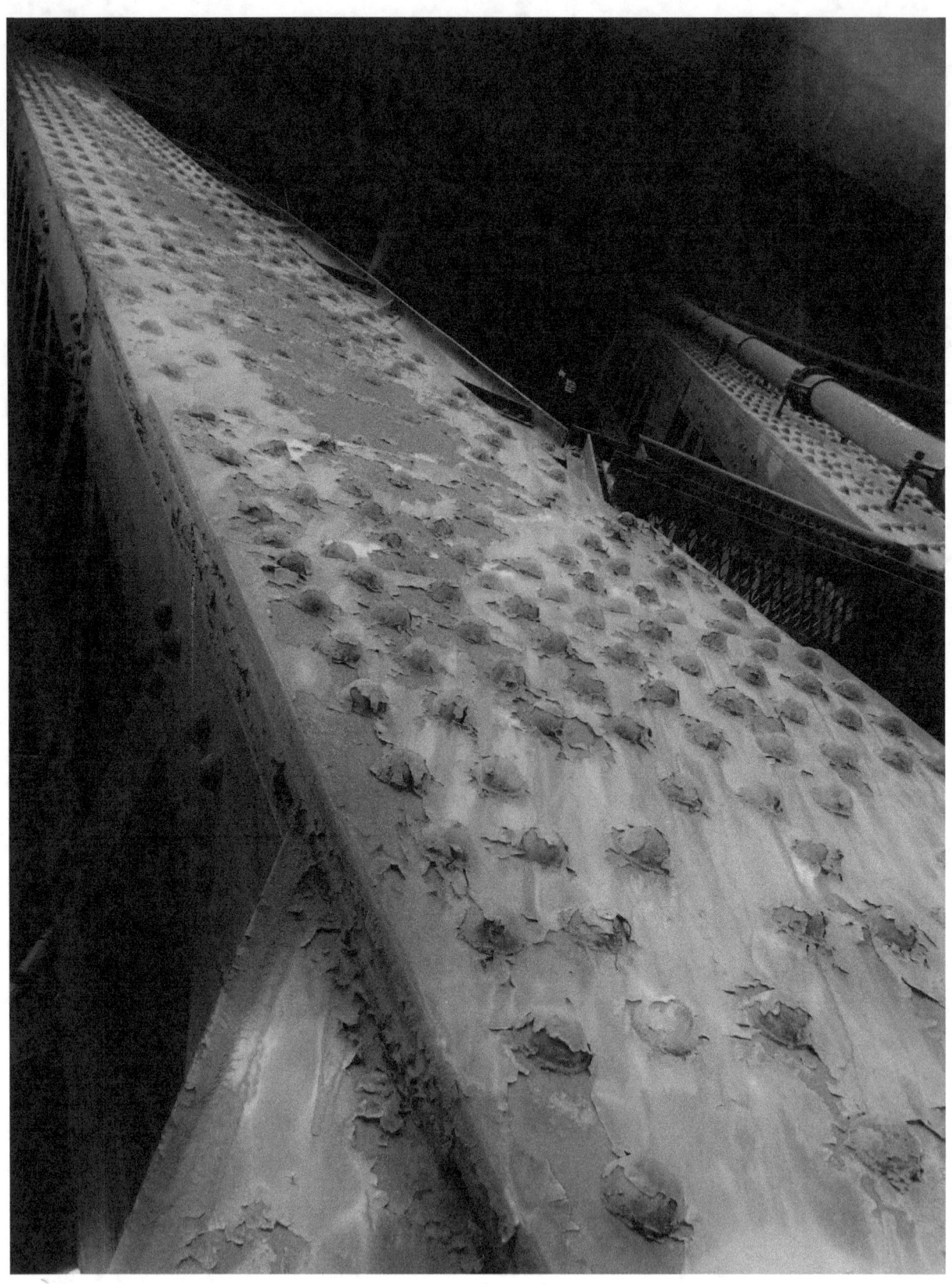

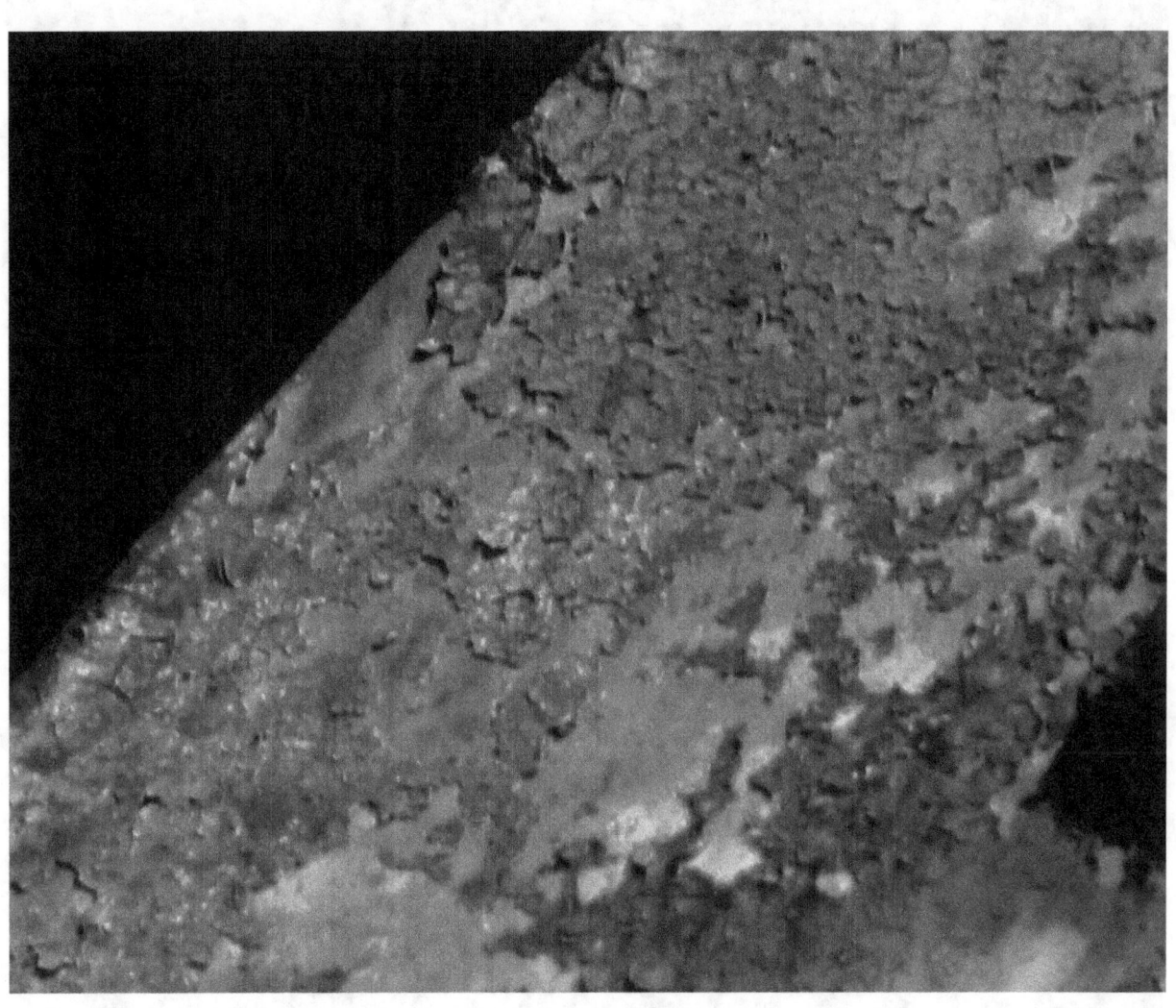

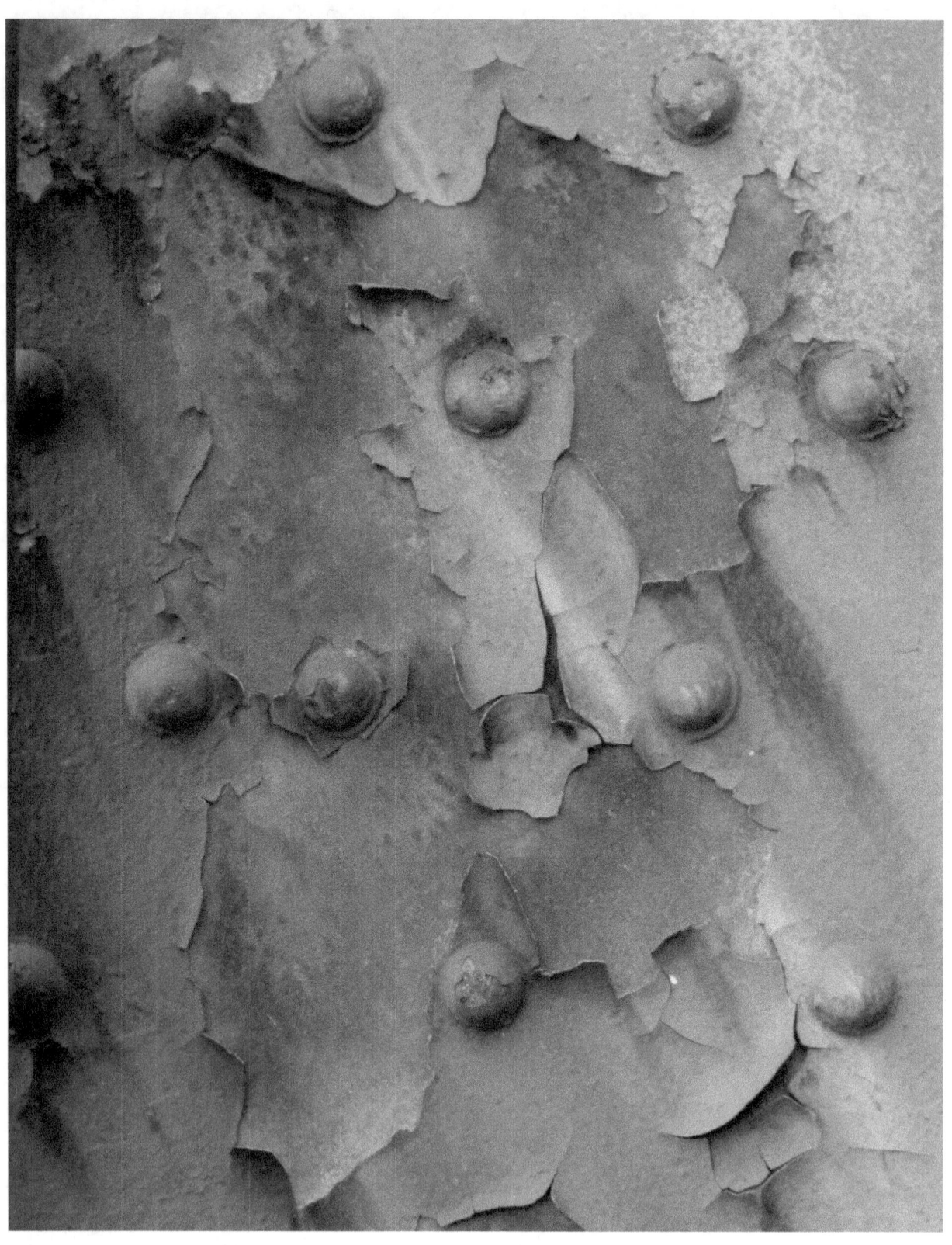

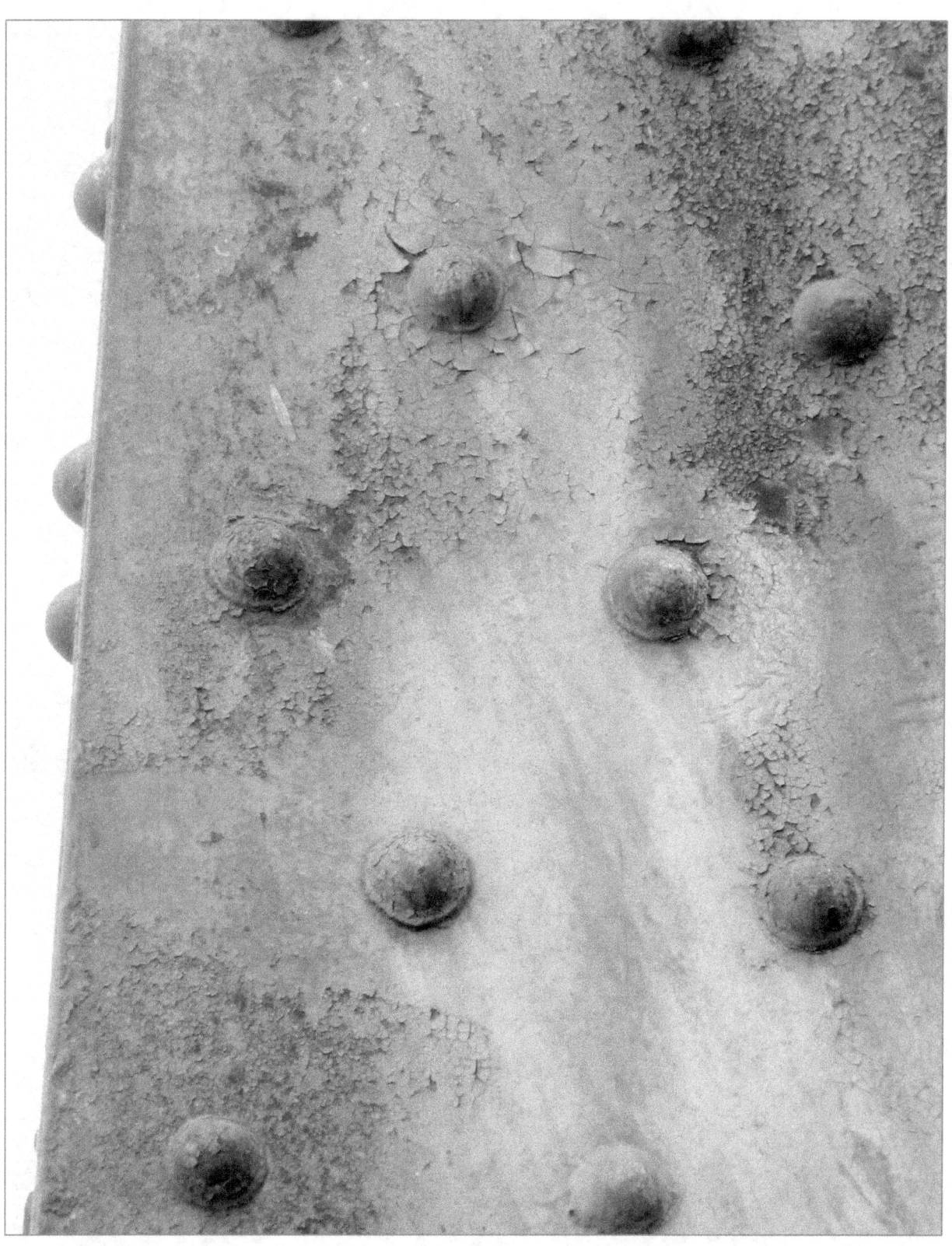

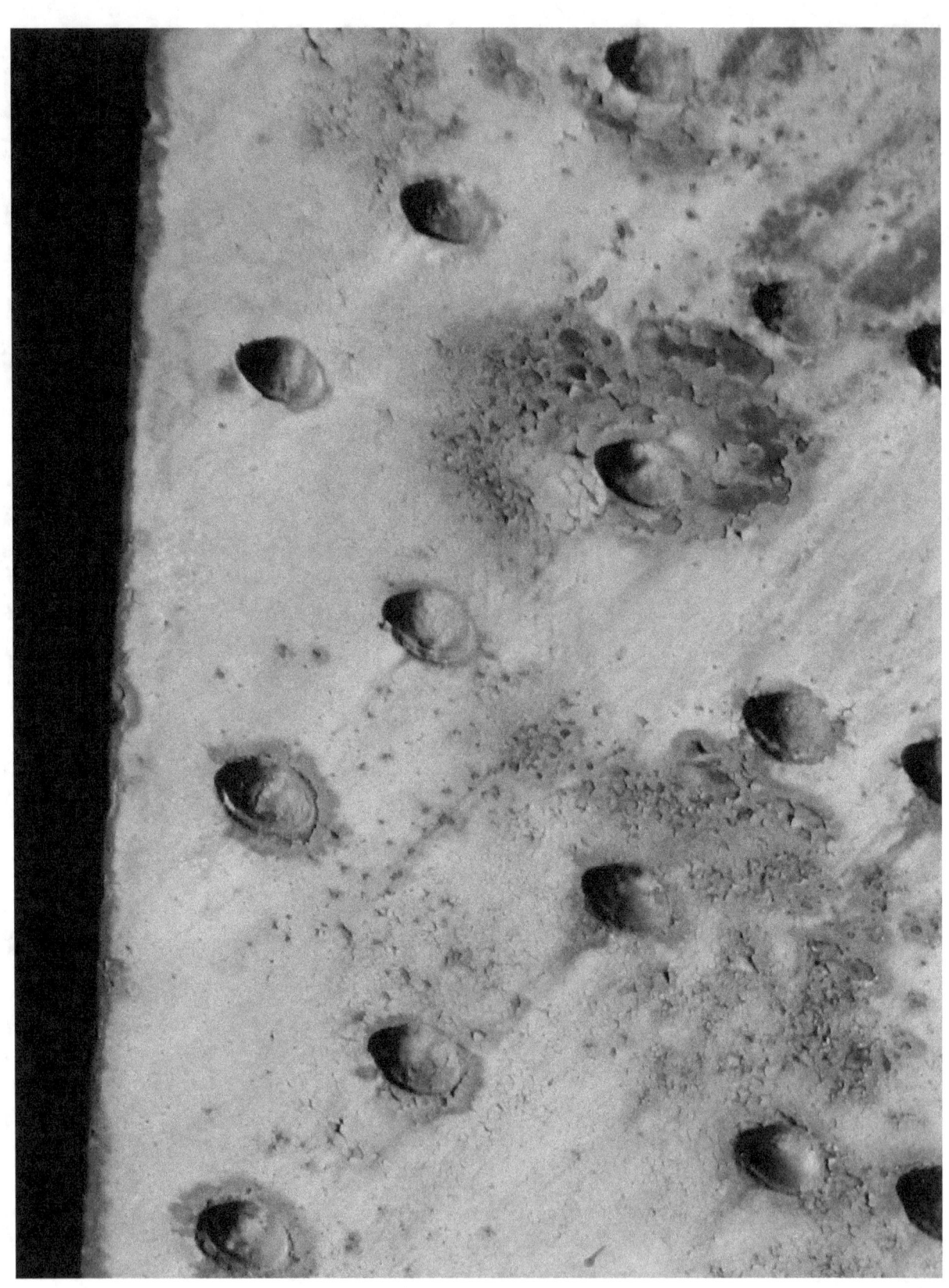

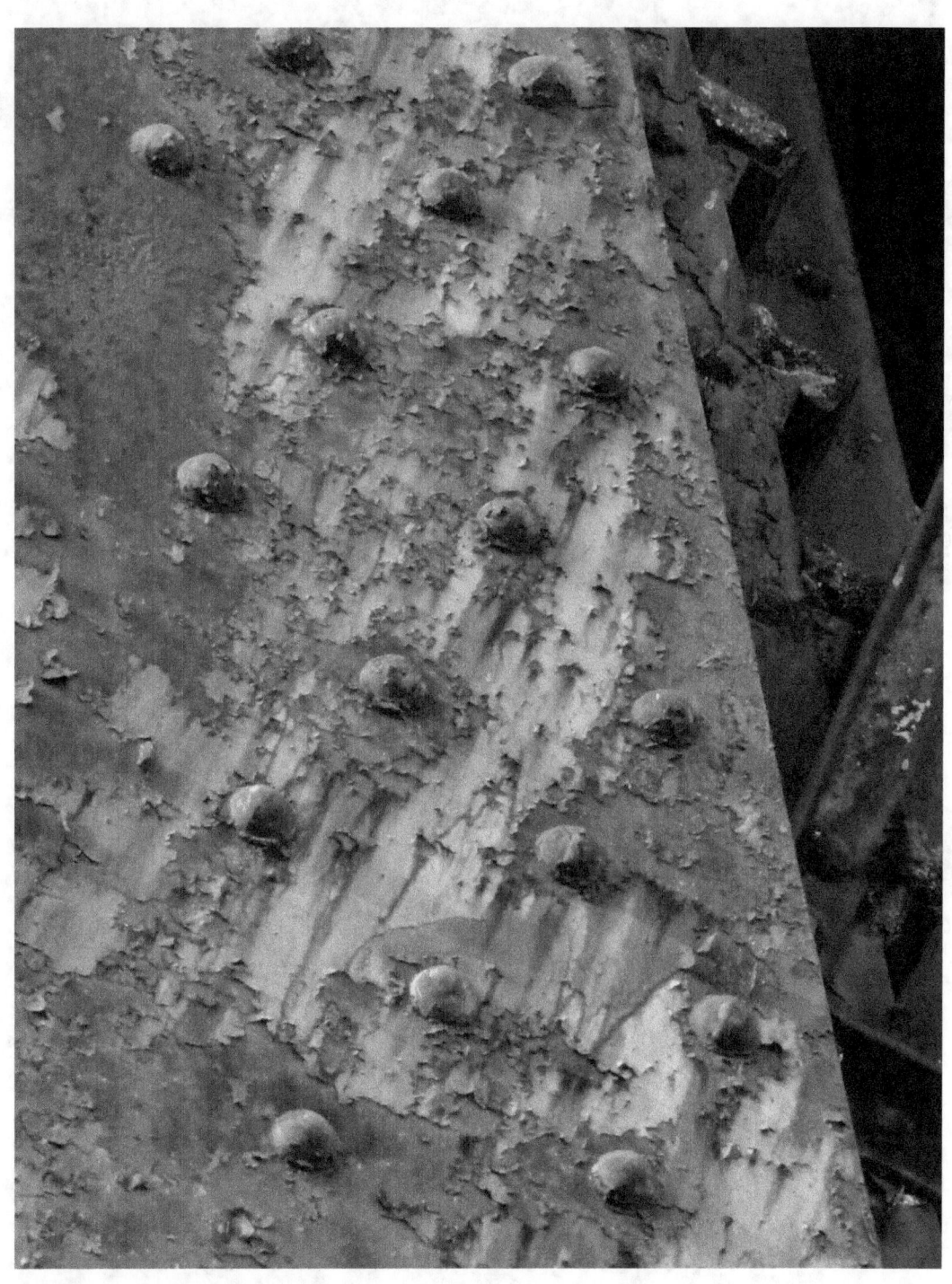

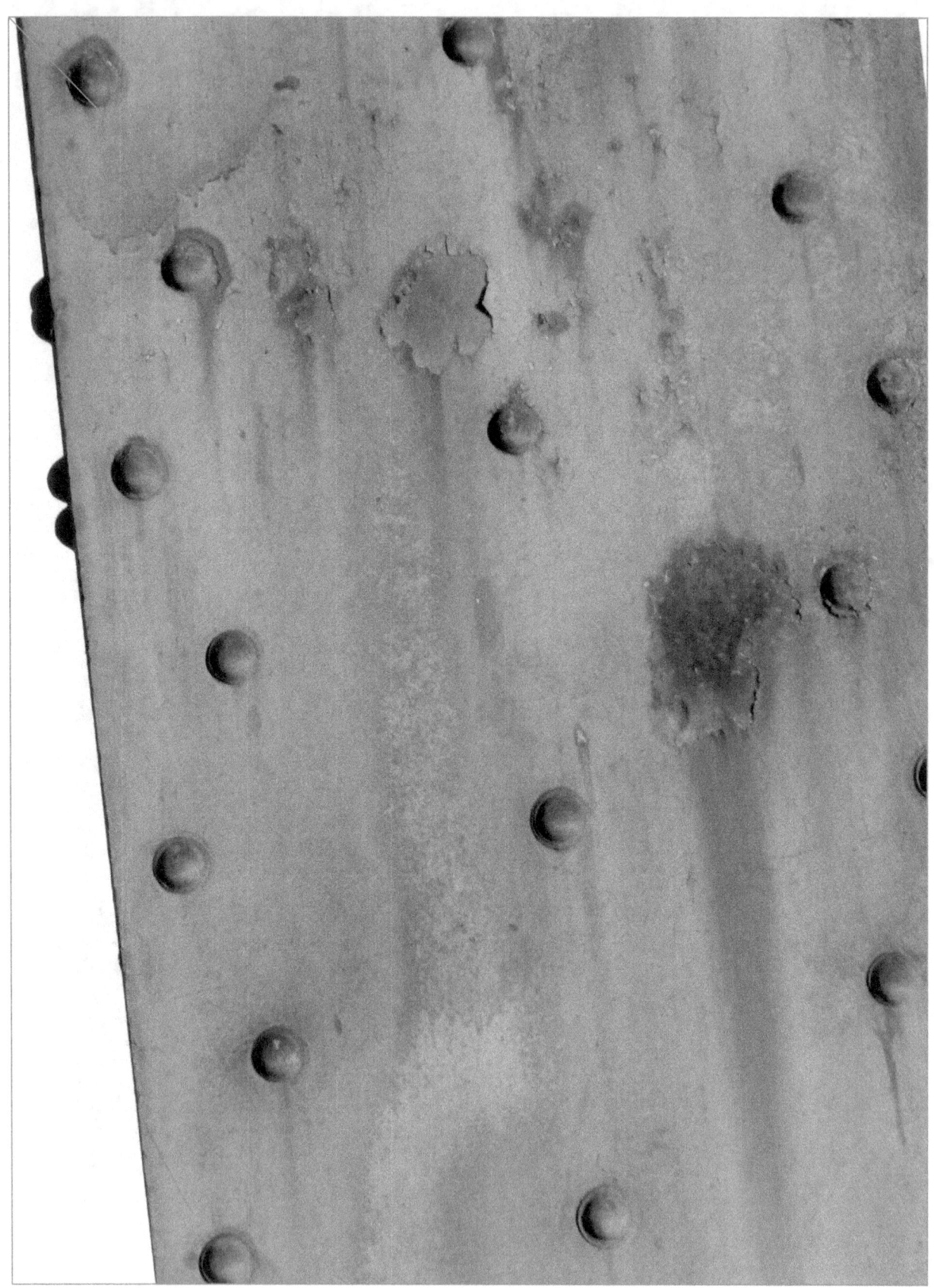

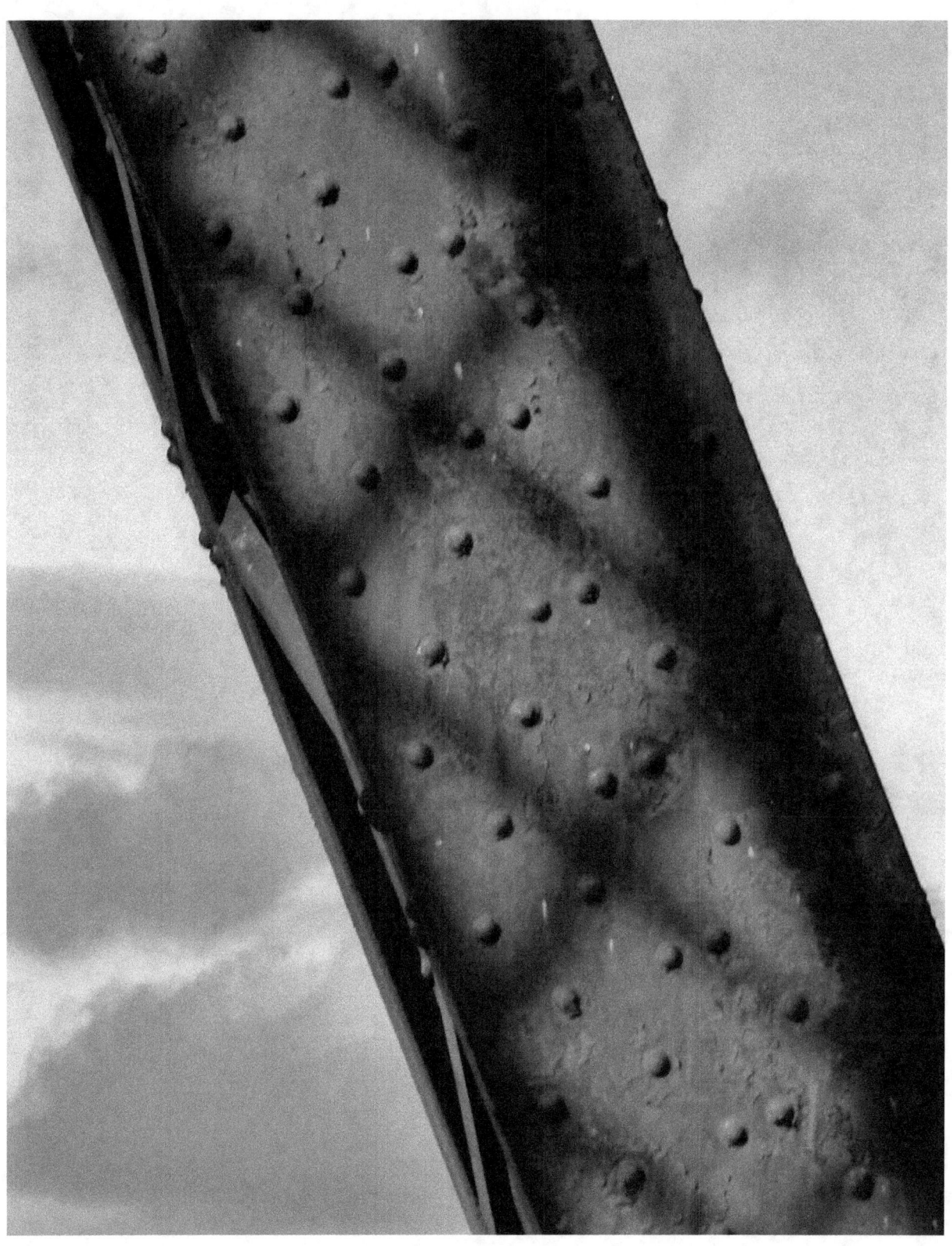

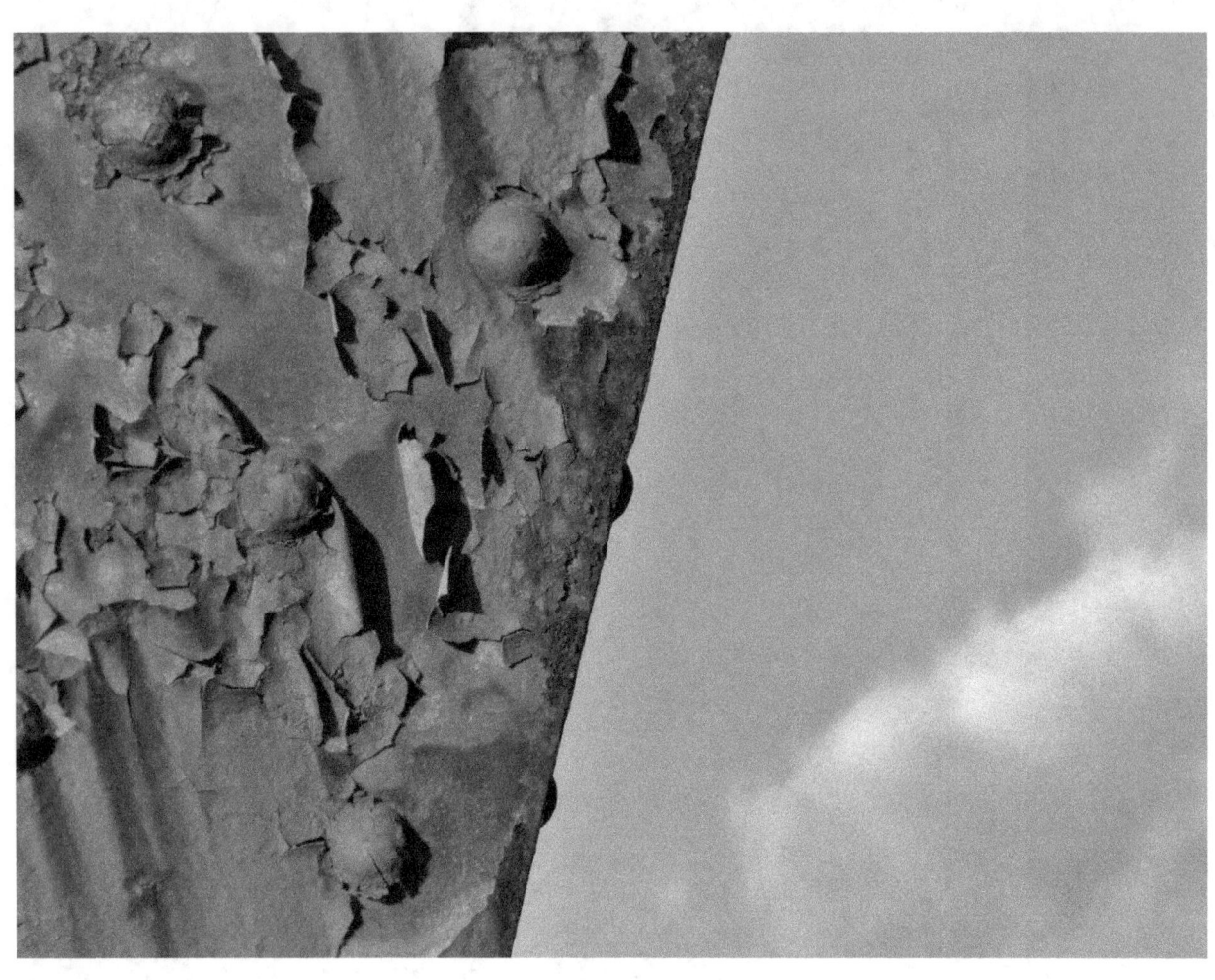

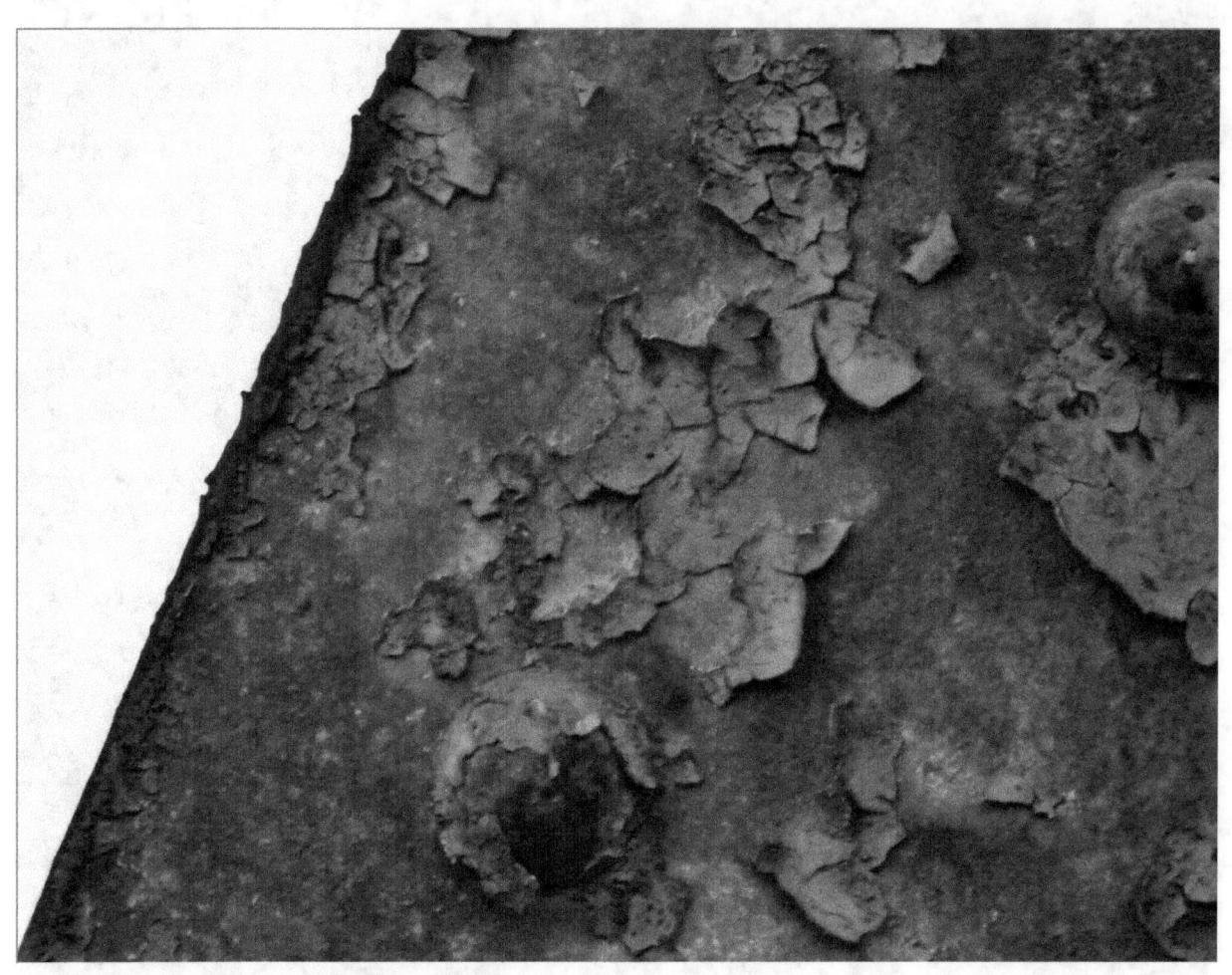

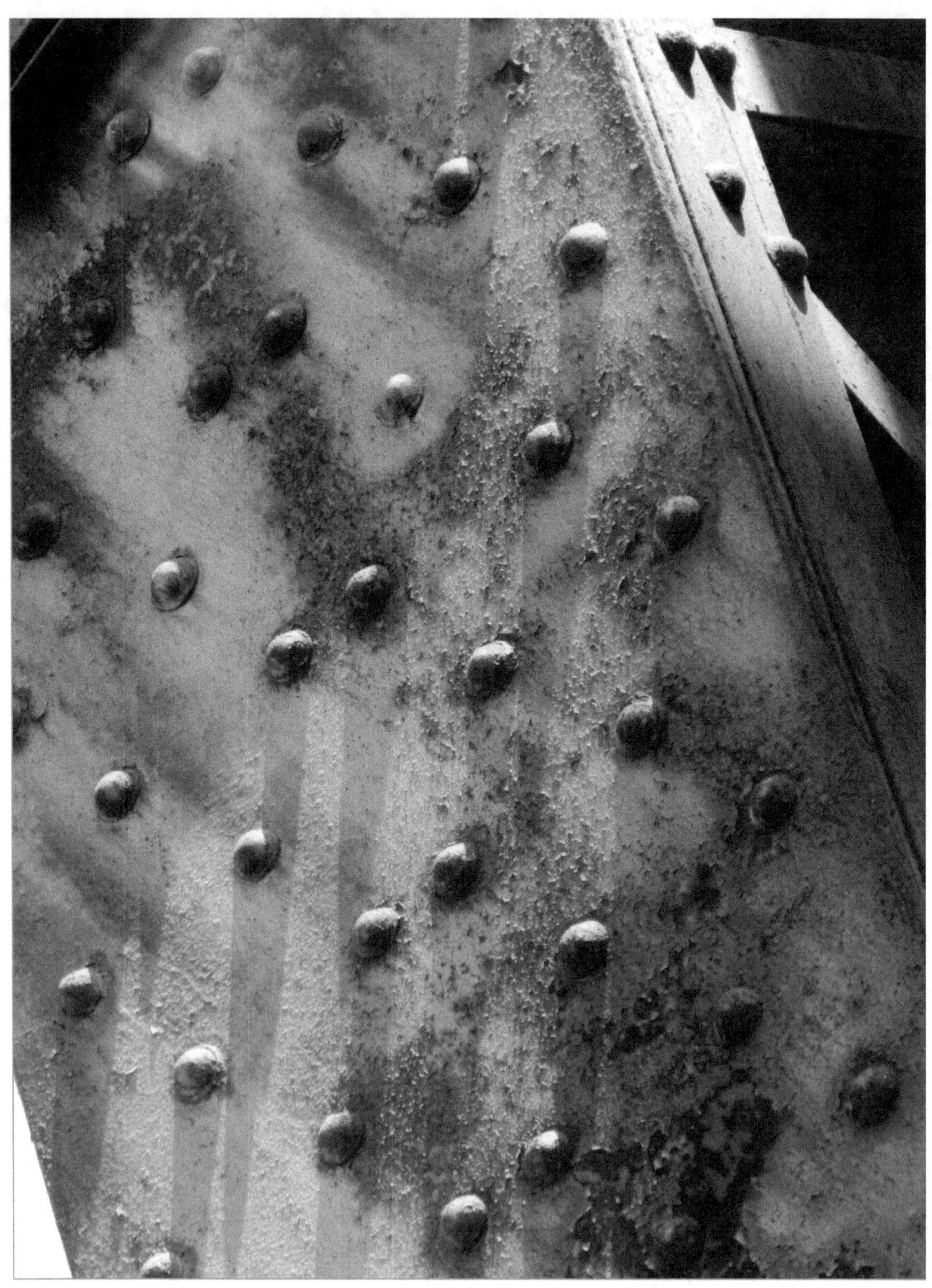

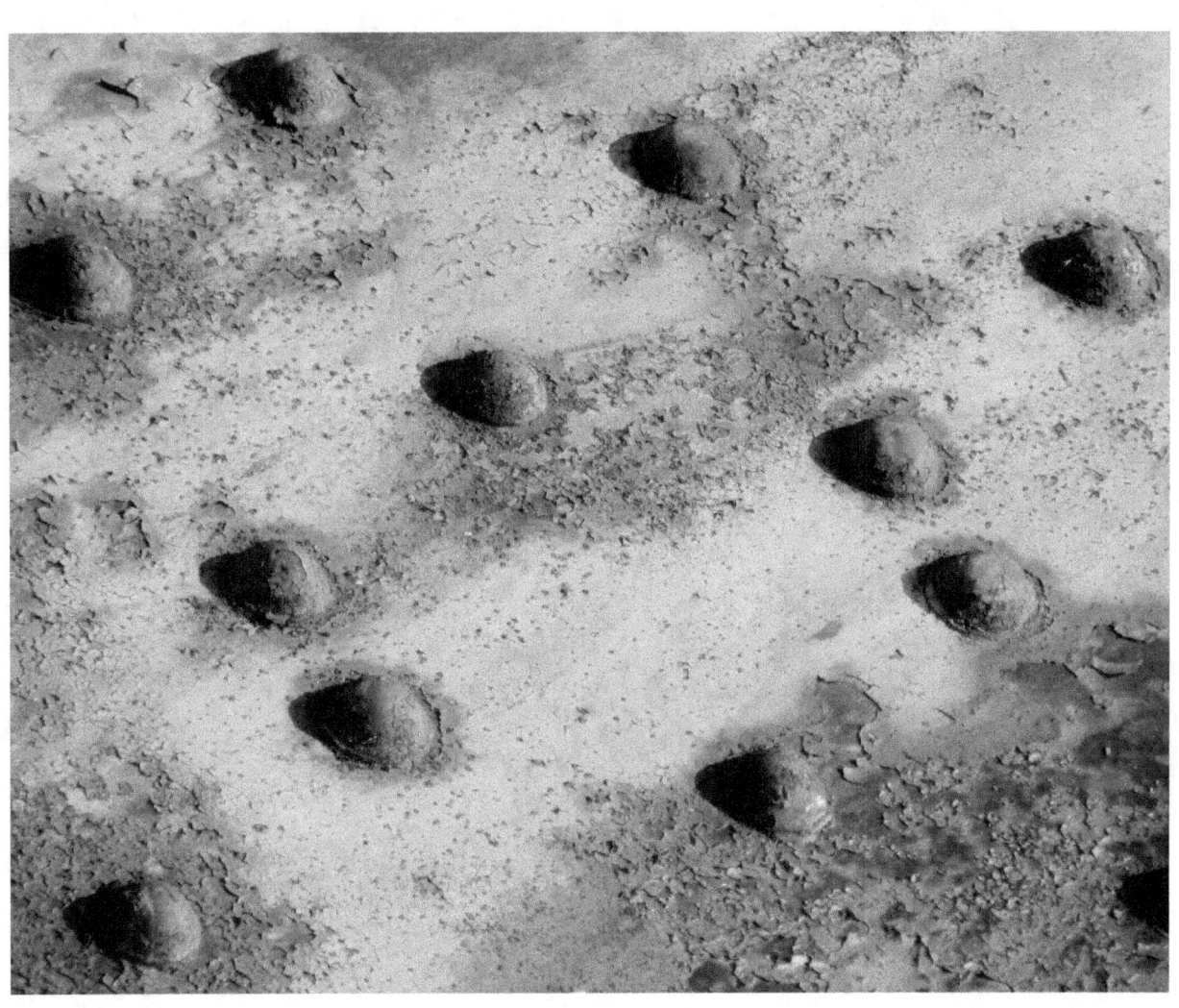

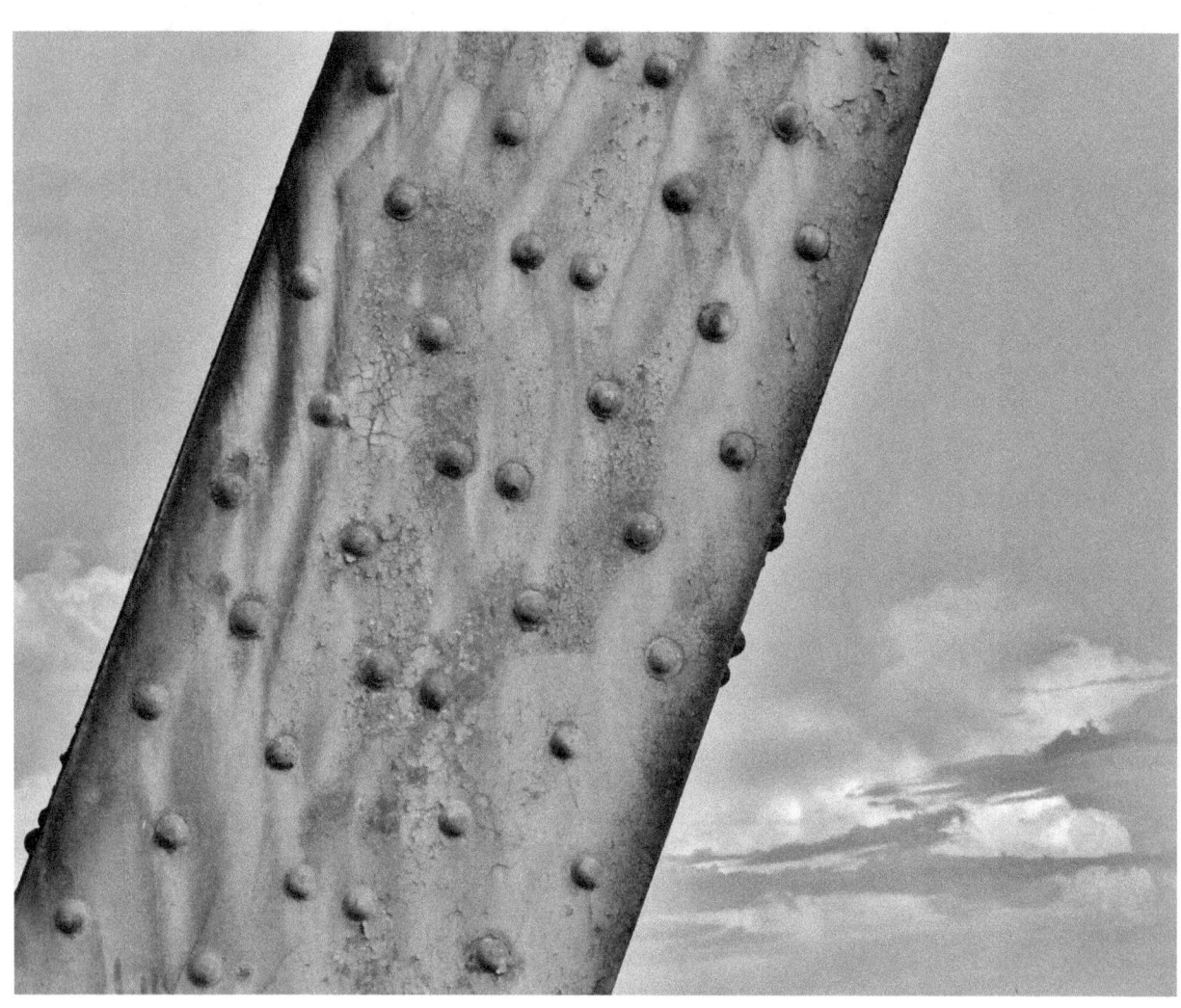

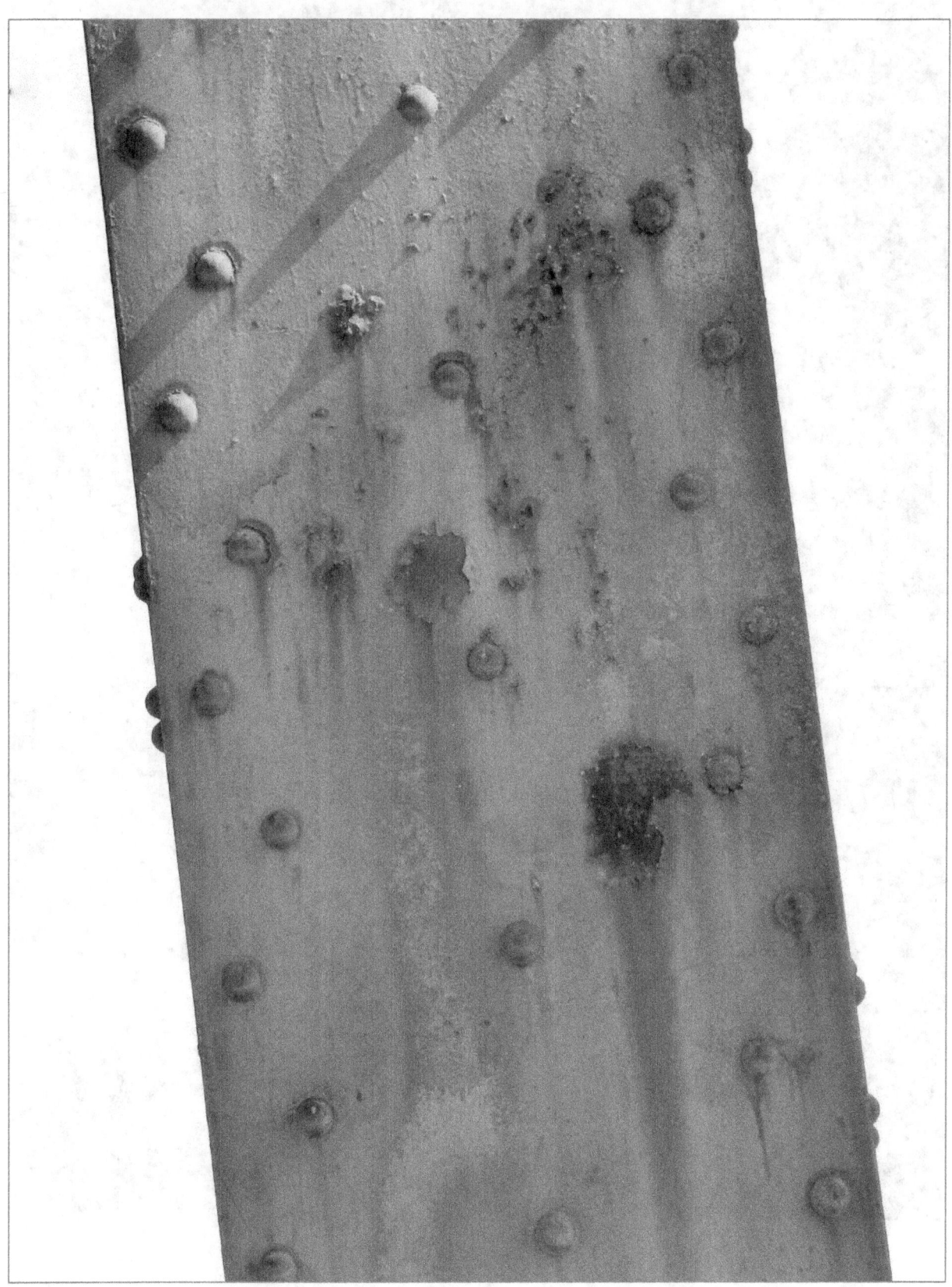

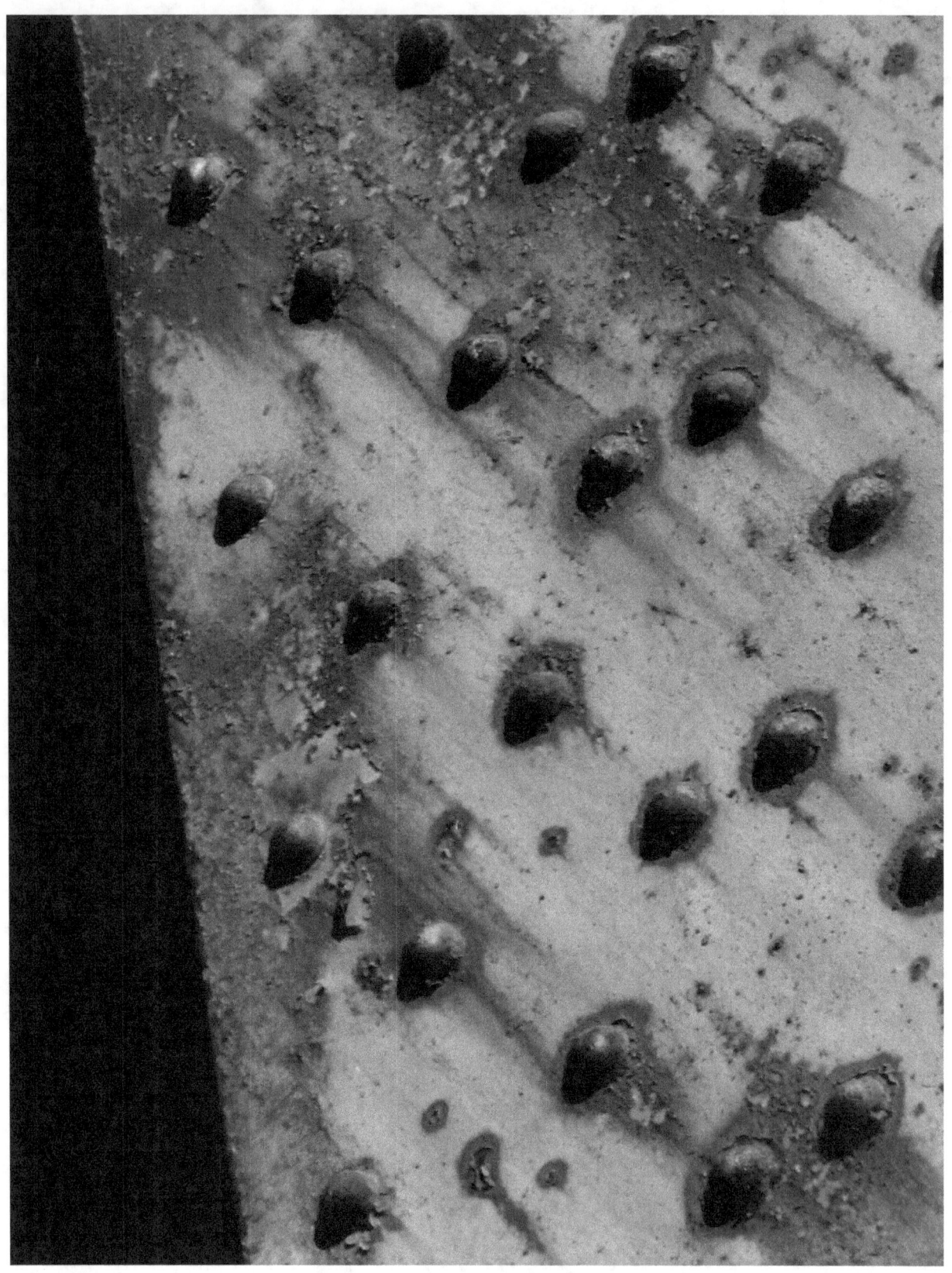

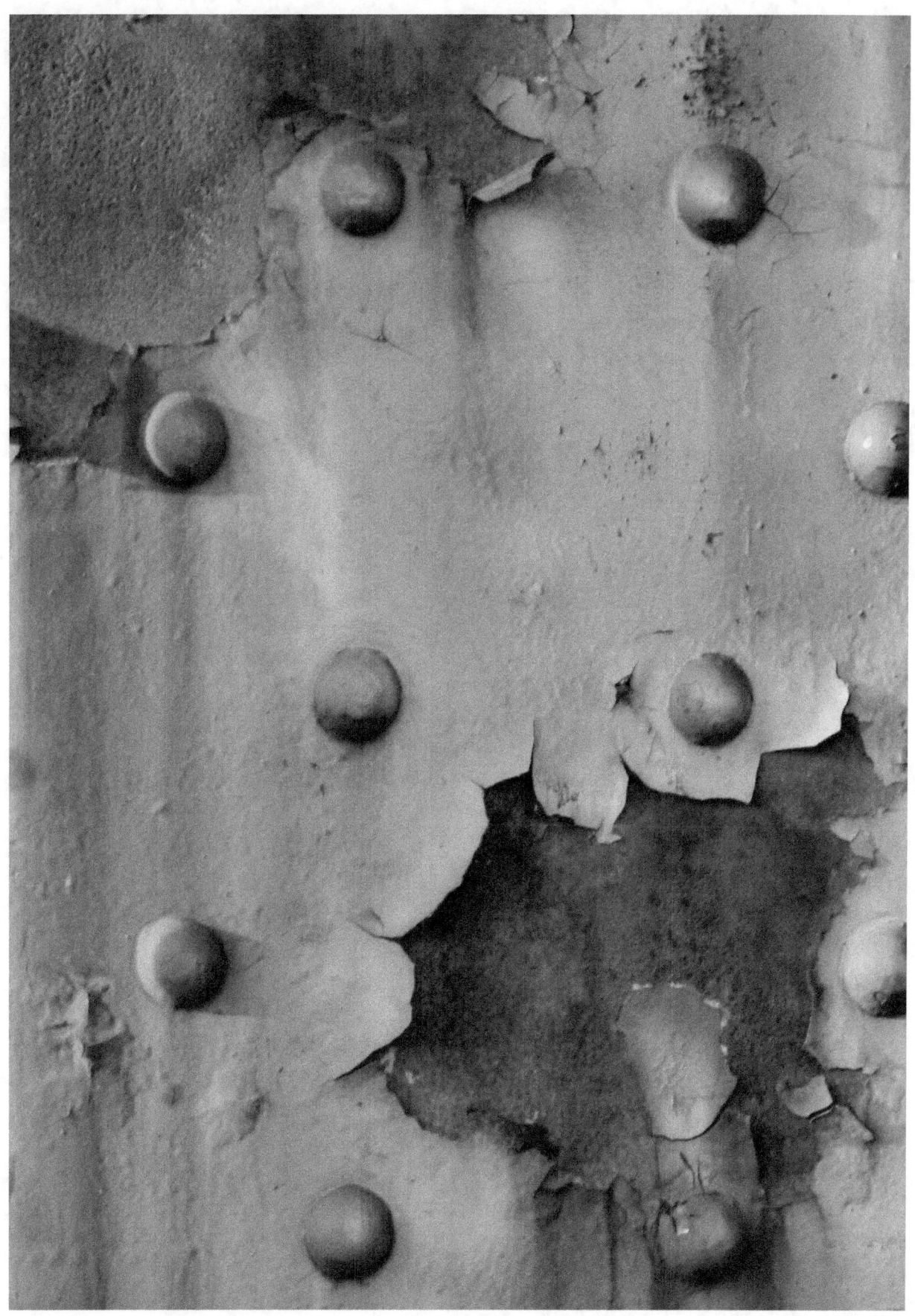

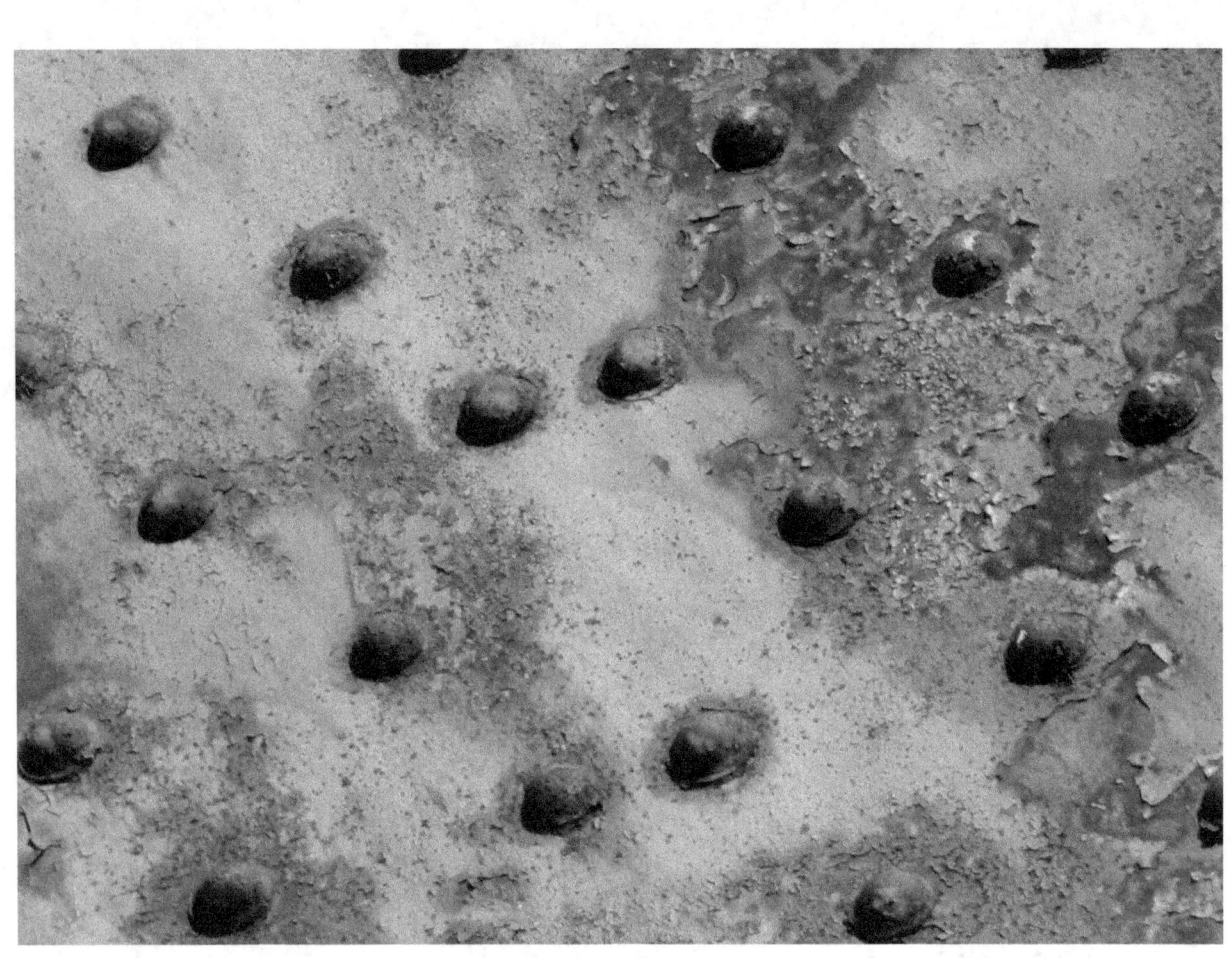

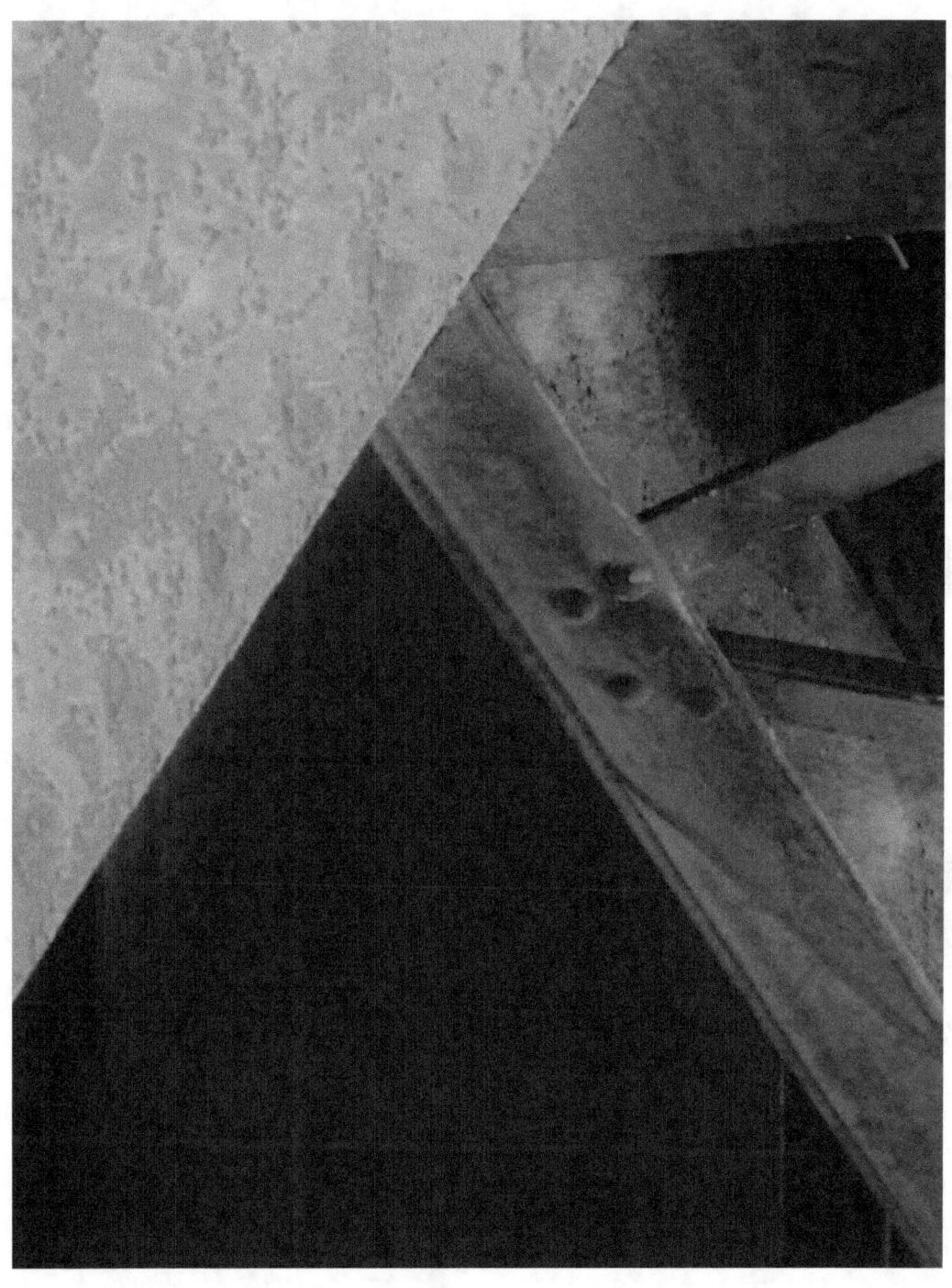

About the Photographer

Charles Lucas was born in Kentucky, raised in Chicago, and lives in Portland, Oregon.